EDGAR JOHNSON GOODSPEED

SOCIETY OF BIBLICAL LITERATURE
BIBLICAL SCHOLARSHIP IN NORTH AMERICA

Robert W. Funk
and
Kent Harold Richards
Editors

NUMBER 4
EDGAR JOHNSON GOODSPEED
Articulate Scholar

James I. Cook

JAMES I. COOK

EDGAR JOHNSON GOODSPEED
Articulate Scholar

SCHOLARS PRESS

Distributed by
Scholars Press
101 Salem Street
P.O. Box 2268
Chico, California 95927

The Society of Biblical Literature gratefully acknowledges a grant from the National Endowment for the Humanities to underwrite certain editorial and research expenses of the Centennial Publications Series. Published results and interpretations do not necessarily represent the view of the Endowment.

Library of Congress Cataloging in Publication Data

Cook, James I.
    Edgar Johnson Goodspeed, articulate scholar

    (Biblical scholarship in North America ; no. 4)
    Includes bibliographical references.
    "A classified list of Edgar J. Goodspeed's books and pamphlets with annotations": p.
    "A list of the publications of Edgar J. Goodspeed": p
    1. Goodspeed, Edgar Johnson, 1871–1962. 2. New Testament scholars—United States—Biography. I. Title. II. Series.
BS2351.G6C66   225   80–21070
ISBN 0–89130–439–8 pbk.

Printed in the United States of America
1   2   3   4   5
Edwards Brothers, Inc.
Ann Arbor, Michigan 48106

TO JEAN
συγκληρονόμος χάριτος ζωῆς

TABLE OF CONTENTS

INTRODUCTION

In the long and painstaking process of human learning, no man is an island. The accumulation of knowledge is a vast cooperative undertaking that spans the centuries and continents incorporating the labors of innumerable scholars. Within this general process every field of specialization has its place. Thus, in the area of New Testament research, each generation does not begin anew but rather stands upon the shoulders of its predecessor. It is this historical and investigational continuity which not only makes progress possible but also places upon each generation the obligation to acknowledge and to weigh their predecessors' contributions. Perhaps more quickly than colleagues in other disciplines, the biblical student finds a personal application in the words, "others have labored, and you have entered into their labor."

A New Testament scholar whose remarkable labor spanned the first half of the twentieth century was Edgar J. Goodspeed. He was an influential teacher, an able scholar and a prolific author. The reader of books dealing with the New Testament and early Christian literature encounters references to Goodspeed's work under a bewildering variety of titles and headings. A volume which demonstrates this fact to an unusual degree is *The Study of the Bible Today and Tomorrow.*[1] The several contributors find cause to cite or refer to Goodspeed in such essays as "Intertestamental Studies since Charles's Apocrypha and Pseudepigrapha,"[2] "New Testament Criticism in the World-Wars Period,"[3] "Urgent Tasks for New Testament Research,"[4] "Reassessing the Religious Importance of Paul,"[5] "The Emergence of the Church in the Pre-Catholic Period,"[6] and "A Critique of the Revised Standard Version of the New Testament."[7] If some allowance must be made for special interest in this Chicago volume, the solid core of widely respected Goodspeed publications remains. The breadth of his work, however, is not a matter which rests upon a foundation of parochial interpretation. In their surveys of New Testament

---

[1] Ed. H. R. Willoughby (Chicago: University of Chicago Press, 1947).
[2] Ibid., J. C. Rylaarsdam, 36.
[3] Ibid., M. M. Parvis, 66, 69.
[4] Ibid., P. Schubert, 217n.
[5] Ibid., D. W. Riddle, 314n.
[6] Ibid., S. E. Johnson, 359n.
[7] Ibid., A. P. Wikgren, 385n., *et passim.*

studies, W. F. Howard,[8] A. M. Hunter[9] and F. V. Filson[10] take remarkably
diverse notice of Goodspeed's endeavors. His translation of the New Testament and of the Apocrypha assures him a place in the histories of English
versions.[11] J. Quasten makes a number of references to Goodspeed's publications in the field of patristics and states concerning the text of the Greek
Apologists: "The best edition is E. J. Goodspeed, *Die ältesten Apologeten.*
Göttingen, 1914; it includes all the second-century Apologists except
Theophilus."[12]

In spite of these widespread citations of Goodspeed's work in various
fields and the fact that a leading religious journalist did not hesitate to de-
scribe him as "America's greatest New Testament scholar,"[13] there has been
no adequate attempt either to acknowledge or to measure the significance of
his major contributions to New Testament research. There are only brief
and scattered references. W. G. Kümmel, for example, does not so much as
mention Goodspeed in his history of the investigation of New Testament
problems.[14] With the exception of his Ephesian hypothesis, which continues
to enjoy adherents in Great Britain, Goodspeed appears to have been largely
ignored on the other side of the Atlantic. To what extent this represents a
fair judgment on the value of his work and to what extent it results from a
tendency to prejudge any non-German scholarship as insignificant are difficult to assess. That this scholarly provincialism is no respecter of persons
may be judged from a comment of W. F. Howard on the Four-Document
theory of B. H. Streeter: "Perhaps because of its English origin it has never

[8] *The Romance of New Testament Scholarship* (London: The Epworth Press, 1949). In his
chapter on "The Papyrologists" Howard writes: "It would take too long to recite the names of
all the universities and libraries which have published transcriptions and commentaries on collections which have passed into their possession, though honorable mention should be made of
the work done by Professor E. J. Goodspeed of Chicago" (115).

[9] *Interpreting the New Testament*, 1900–1950 (London: SCM Press, 1951). Hunter suggests
that in his New Testament translation Goodspeed "did for American readers what Moffatt had
done for the people in this country" (9). Again, his survey of twentieth-century Pauline studies
takes note of Goodspeed's Ephesian hypothesis (63).

[10] "The Study of the New Testament," *Protestant Thought in the Twentieth Century*, ed.
A. S. Nash (New York: The Macmillan Company, 1951). After pointing out Goodspeed's role in
the Aramiac-Hellenistic debate, Filson continues: "But his chief claim to present recognition is
not in this point, nor in his half-century of activity in American manuscript study, but in his
view of the origin of Ephesians" (56).

[11] E.g., H. Pope, *English Versions of the Bible* (St. Louis, Missouri: B. Herder Book Co.,
1951).

[12] *Patrology*, I (Westminster, Maryland: The Newman Press, 1950) 189. Cf. also the comment
of B. M. Metzger, "Goodspeed, Edgar Johnson," *Die Religion in Geschichte und Gegenwart*, II
(3te Aufl.; Tübingen: J. C. B. Mohr, 1958) 1693: "Wertvoll sind sein Index Patristicus (1907)
und Index Apologeticus (1912)." The continuing value of Goodspeed's *Index Patristicus* is evi-
denced by the fact that it was reprinted with corrections in 1960 (Naperville: A. R. Allenson).

[13] Harold E. Fey, *Saturday Review of Literature* 23 (December 23, 1950) 9.

[14] *The New Testament: The History of the Investigation of Its Problems* (Nashville: Abing-
don Press, 1972).

won great favour in Germany, and I might add that I was told many years ago that, because of its Oxford parentage, it had not won complete favour in Cambridge."[15] If this continental attitude is substantial enough to be sensed in Great Britain, how much more so by the scholars of the New World! In a candid examination of the situation, F. V. Filson stated in 1952 that a

> notable feature Protestant New Testament study in America has been its constant reflection of European trends. This has always been true and remains true today. . . . Perhaps American Biblical scholarship has at times needed more originality and independence. But it is a partial compensation that the originality, which has not been lacking, has worked against a background of acquaintance with the best scholarship of other countries.[16]

A thorough review of the scholarly preparation and productivity of Goodspeed suggests that these words are a reasonably accurate description of his place in American New Testament scholarship. He combined an early acquaintance with, and respect for, the best continental investigators with a generous measure of originality. If it should be argued that Goodspeed has not merited international notice because his most significant contributions were made within the context of American biblical studies, there is, then, all the more reason for an American recognition and evaluation of his work. Until now, however, nothing has been published beyond a brief biography and a bibliography of Goodspeed's publications prior to 1948.[17] The present work has been undertaken to fill this gap in the history of the contribution of American scholarship to New Testament research.

Because Goodspeed's family background and early environment provide unusually helpful insights into his later development, a sketch of the most pertinent facts and formative factors involved is presented first. This is followed by chapters dealing with his contribution to New Testament studies in five areas. In this way it becomes possible to gain an overall view of his productivity. The size, variety and uneven value of this literature establishes the need to be selective and representative for purposes of critical evaluation. His Ephesian hypothesis and its implications for the formation of the Pauline corpus and the New Testament, his New Testament translation, his translation of the Apocrypha and related contributions to studies in apocryphal literature,

[15] "A Survey of New Testament Studies during Half a Century," *The London Quarterly and Holborn Review* 177 (1952) 11.

[16] "The Study of the New Testament," 48–49.

[17] J. H. Cobb and L. B. Jennings, *A Biography and Bibliography of Edgar Johnson Goodspeed* (Chicago: University of Chicago Press, 1948). Notice may also be taken of two doctoral dissertations: G. W. Barker, "A Critical Evaluation of the Lexical and Linguistic Data Advanced by E. J. Goodspeed and Supported by C. L. Mitton in a Proposed Solution to the Problem of the Authorship and Date of Ephesians" (summarized in *HTR* 56 (1963) 87f.); and J. I. Cook, "A Critical Evaluation of the Contributions of Edgar Johnson Goodspeed as a New Testament Scholar," Princeton Theological Seminary, 1963.

and his role in the debate over the Hellenistic versus the Semitic background of the New Testament have been selected as the major areas of his scholarly contribution. His volume on the life of Jesus is included both as the best available expression of his theological views and as the most significant representative of his later biographical studies of New Testament personalities.

If Edgar J. Goodspeed had confined himself to teaching, his influence would have been largely limited to the classroom and to such of his views as his students chose to perpetuate in their own work. To that extent, the evaluation of his contributions would have been made as his teaching career progressed and, for all practical purposes, would have been completed at his retirement. But Goodspeed has been and continues to be a popular translator and author.[18] He is not, therefore, simply a scholar whom another generation of students met in the classroom; he is an author encountered by the public in bookstores. He is not only a figure of the past; he is an influence of the present and, as such, deserves to be known as a person and acknowledged as a scholar.

Moreover, Goodspeed was an active participant in biblical studies for nearly half a century. He pioneered vigorously for the modern speech movement in New Testament translation. He argued for the return of the Apocrypha in versions of the English Bible and to that end both translated and wrote. He challenged the proponents of the theory that written Aramaic originals underlie much of the Greek New Testament and contributed a brilliant hypothesis to the discussion concerning the origin of Ephesians.

Finally, there is value in drawing attention to a scholar who made a determined effort to communicate the progress of scientific biblical research to the intelligent general reader. Whether Goodspeed would have done this in any event cannot be determined, but it is clear that the chief motivation for this effort was provided by the public reception of his New Testament translation. In an address delivered at the Opening Exercises of the Divinity School of the University of Chicago in 1926, he spoke of the significant advances that had been made for New Testament study in the areas of Greek papyri, grammars, lexicons and the canon:

---

[18] His obituary notice in *Publisher's Weekly* 181 (January 29, 1962) 97, for example, testifies with the eloquence of statistics to his literary impact. Observing that he is the author of more than fifty books, the notice continues: "The University of Chicago published some 43 of Dr. Goodspeed's books. The bestselling titles among them, all of which are in print, are the Bible, an American translation by Dr. Goodspeed and J. M. Powis Smith, which was published in 1935 and has sold 229,000 copies; the Complete Bible of which Dr. Goodspeed translated the New Testament and the Apocrypha, published in 1939, which has sold 186,000 copies; the New Testament (1923, 220,000 copies); 'An Introduction to the New Testament' (1937, 27,000 copies); 'The Story of the Bible' (1936, 67,000); 'The Story of the New Testament' (1916, 95,000); 'The Story of the Old Testament' (1934, 47,000); 'Goodspeed Parallel New Testament' (1943, 43,000)."

To mediate this new knowledge, this new New Testament, to the Christian
and to the educated public—this is the great task in which we must take our
share. One of the tragedies of the hour is the ignorance of the New Testament on the part of otherwise educated people. This would not matter so
much if they would let it alone, but that is just what they will not do. Essay-
ists, journalists, educators, reformers, and reactionaries—all insist upon dealing with the New Testament. If one seeks to correct them, one simply does
not know where to begin.[19]

Because no one took this charge more seriously than its author, Goodspeed's
technical and scholarly publications were balanced by a sizable number of
volumes intended to mediate the results of biblical research to the educated
public. If communication is a legitimate obligation of scholarship, this contribution of E. J. Goodspeed is worthy of recognition and emulation.

[19] "The Challenge of New Testament Study," *JR* 6 (1926) 526–27.

I
EDGAR JOHNSON GOODSPEED

Edgar Johnson Goodspeed, born October 23, 1871, in Quincy, Illinois, was the younger of two sons of Thomas Wakefield and Mary Ellen (Ten Broeke) Goodspeed. The Goodspeed family had migrated to America from Oxfordshire in the seventeenth century. At the time of Edgar Goodspeed's birth, his father, an eminent member of the Baptist clergy, was giving up his Quincy pastorate to go to the aid of his oldest brother Edgar as an associate in the pastorate of the Second Baptist Church of Chicago. In 1876, after a few years of Chicago residence, the family moved to the suburb of Morgan Park where Thomas W. Goodspeed had taken a position with the Baptist Union Theological Seminary. Relatives who chose to take advantage of the Goodspeed hospitality while attending the schools of Morgan Park discharged their indebtedness by tutoring the Goodspeed boys, Charles and Edgar, two or three hours a day. This arrangement enabled Edgar to begin the study of Latin at the age of ten. The academic atmosphere which pervaded the Goodspeed home was always closely related to the church, and in his eleventh or twelfth year Edgar Goodspeed became a member of the Baptist congregation in Morgan Park. When in 1893 the family moved from Morgan Park to Hyde Park to be near the new University of Chicago, the Goodspeeds all joined the Hyde Park Baptist Church.

Before he had reached his thirteenth year, Goodspeed was preparing for college by attending what is known as the old University of Chicago. There he continued the study of Latin and began his formal training in Greek. He was graduated with the final preparatory class in 1886 and in the same year matriculated at Denison University in Ohio. At Denison he specialized in the classics, played baseball on his class's team, and became president of the Calliopean Literary Society in his senior year. Denison did not award prizes to its students, but Goodspeed "showed best" in Greek, Latin, modern languages and physiology.[1] He was graduated with the A. B. degree in 1890 and in the fall of that year began graduate work at Yale University under William Rainey Harper, a close friend of the Goodspeed family. His courses—Hebrew, Arabic and Old Testament Legal Literature—were all with Harper himself.

During Goodspeed's years at Denison, his father was working to re-establish the University of Chicago. This project gained substantial impetus

---

[1] *Current Biography* (New York: The H. W. Wilson Company, 1946) 215.

when Thomas W. Goodspeed was able to interest John D. Rockefeller in donating funds to this cause. Rockefeller promised a gift of six hundred thousand dollars if four hundred thousand could be raised in addition. Uniting his efforts with those of the secretary of the American Baptist Education Society, Thomas Goodspeed secured the stipulated amount. When the work was done and the first trustees were assembled, the elder Goodspeed was at once elected Secretary of the Board, an office which he retained until his retirement at the age of seventy. He was also one of the six "incorporators" of the University selected by Rockefeller.

After his graduate year at Yale, Goodspeed returned home to take his first job and to continue his graduate studies at the new University of Chicago when it opened its doors in the fall of 1892. The job consisted of teaching beginning Latin and Greek for one year in a tutorial group called the Owen Academy at Morgan Park; the studies represented a continuation of work in Semitics with William R. Harper, who had come to the University of Chicago as its first President. Goodspeed went on in Assyrian with Robert F. Harper, the President's brother, and later took up Syriac and Ethiopic with the President. During his graduate years at Chicago, he taught beginning Greek, Xenophon, and Homer at the South Side Academy. His third graduate year at Chicago was marked by the transfer of his studies to the New Testament field, and it was in this area of specialization that he took his Doctor of Philosophy degree at Chicago in 1898. "Soon after," Goodspeed remembers, "the President informed me that I was to be added to the New Testament department as Assistant, without salary, for two years, when I would begin to receive a thousand dollars a year as an Associate. But I must go abroad for two years to visit the German universities first."[2] He accordingly journeyed to Germany and spent a semester at Berlin, taking in Adolf Harnack's lectures, and working on Greek papyri under Fritz Krebs. These studies were followed by a tour of the major universities and libraries of Europe, and visits with the leading authorities in various linguistic and biblical fields. Notable among these contacts was a meeting with Bernard Grenfell and Arthur Hunt, which later resulted in Goodspeed's having a share in the editing of the Tebtunis papyri. Visits to Egypt and the Holy Land completed the tour. Fifty years later, Goodspeed summarized the value of this experience as follows:

> As I sailed for home after two solid years abroad, what had they given me? A wider and more immediate knowledge of scholarly personnel and opinion, German and English, for one thing. Closer acquaintance with the Greek papyrus documents of ancient life, for another. A working alliance with Grenfell and Hunt, for a third. Wider social experience, and fuller mastery of familiar spoken English, for a fourth—no small matter, though many

[2] *As I Remember* (New York: Harper & Brothers, 1953) 95.

translators seem to think so! And a firsthand acquaintance with the Holy Land which is, of course, the first and greatest commentary on the Bible.[3]

In the months between his return from abroad and the assumption of his teaching career at the University, Goodspeed became engaged to Elfleda Bond, daughter of the head of the American Radiator Company. Their marriage took place on December 3, 1901.

Edgar Goodspeed's professional association with the University of Chicago was marked by teaching, publication, and administration. Having begun as an instructor in 1902, he had advanced to the rank of full professor by 1915. A former student and colleague has described his teaching ability in these words:

> His method was sheer genius. His classes were utterly informal. He would bring some half dozen books to which he planned to refer, and a manila envelope containing his notes. Some of these notes, the student could see, were written on pieces of old University calendars; they were of varying size, clipped to the area needed for the note. Of course they were constantly brought up to date. They stimulated his thought, and immediately he would launch into a spontaneous conversation so full of interest as to fascinate his students. Informal though the sessions were, the end of the Quarter always found the subject fully and thoroughly covered.

> Whatever the subject matter—textual criticism, the canon, one or another aspect of patristic literature, or the synoptic problem—students were stimulated to work at the question involved, and every aspect of it was illuminated from items of Mr. Goodspeed's own experience. No finer example of scholarship could be set than was made alive every day in his classes.

> This value judgment is not mere opinion. Mr. Goodspeed was chairman of the Department of New Testament and Early Christian Literature for thirteen years. In that period the Department presented thirty-nine candidates for the doctor's degree. This was an inevitable result of the teaching in the Department; students were constantly challenged to contribute to knowledge. For example, one day Mr. Goodspeed brought to class a carton full of manuscripts which he had just received from a dealer. Each student was given one, and assigned the task of reporting next day what he had been able to ascertain of its paleography, handwriting, content, and type of text. During his chairmanship the Department maintained a dozen active research projects, from which came many subjects for degrees.[4]

The responsibility of a scholar to publish was embraced by Goodspeed from the outset of his career. Beginning with such early technical publications as *Greek Papyri from the Cairo Museum* (1902) and *Index Patristicus*

---

[3] Ibid., 115.
[4] D. W. Riddle, "Edgar J. Goodspeed," *University of Chicago Magazine* (March, 1962) 31–32.

(1907), a steady stream of books and articles flowed from his pen, now independently, now in collaboration with other scholars. While serving as President of the Society of Biblical Literature and Exegesis in 1919, he challenged the Aramaic hypothesis of Charles C. Torrey[5] and for two decades led the Hellenistic side of the debate. In the summer of 1920, Harry Pratt Judson invited Goodspeed to take the office of Secretary to the President. Reluctant as he was to turn aside into administration, he accepted and served the University in this way for four years. In the busyness of these very years, Goodspeed found time to prepare and publish his American translation of the New Testament, by far the best seller of the University of Chicago Press.[6] The year of its appearance, 1923, marked Goodspeed's appointment to the chairmanship of the New Testament department. Four years later, on one of his periodic European tours, he discovered the codex of the New Testament that was brought to the University of Chicago and published under the title *The Rockefeller McCormick New Testament* (1932). From 1930 onward he served as a member of the American Standard Bible Committee, thus sharing in the preparation of the Revised Standard Version of the New Testament (1946). These scholarly attainments were officially recognized by the University in 1933 when Goodspeed was designated as the Ernest Dewitt Burton Distinguished Service Professor of the University of Chicago. It was during this period that he was elaborating and publishing his Ephesian hypothesis. In 1937, the year of his retirement, he climaxed his Chicago years with the publication of *An Introduction to the New Testament*.

In addition to the numerous books written during his nearly three and a half decades at Chicago, Goodspeed left other tangible and intangible marks of his influence on the University. *The Rockefeller McCormick New Testament* served as a magnet by which unknown manuscripts were attracted to the library. At this point Goodspeed's powerful influence in the University and his acquaintance with wealthy Chicagoans resulted in the purchase of many of these documents for humanistic research. The progress thus made is dramatized by the fact that when Goodspeed took his degree, the University owned one New Testament manuscript; now its collection (which bears Goodspeed's name) is estimated to be second in America only to the collection of the University of Michigan. In retrospect, the University's memorial acknowledges his "enduring contributions to the University's fame, the permanent values of the manuscripts collection, the lasting worth of the many published volumes, and most of all the impetus to the extension of knowledge by his students now scholars in their own right."[7]

[5] "The Origin of Acts," *JBL* 39 (1920) 83–101.

[6] J. H. Cobb and L. B. Jennings, *A Biography and Bibliography of Edgar Johnson Goodspeed* (Chicago: University of Chicago Press, 1948) 3.

[7] Riddle, "Edgar J. Goodspeed," 32.

Official retirement from his duties at the University of Chicago did not result in a slackened scholarly pace. He moved to Bel-Air, Los Angeles, California, and immediately established a fruitful academic relationship with the University of California at Los Angeles. He lectured there during the academic years 1938–42 and again in the summers of 1945–48. Between the two California assignments he gave the Richard Lectures at the University of Virginia (1939) and was lecturer in biblical literature at Scripps College (1941–42). During these years he was also the recipient of additional academic honors. Denison University, which had previously conferred upon him the A.B. (1890) and the D.D. (1928) degrees, added a Doctor of Letters in 1941. The same year the University of Redlands honored him with the degree of L.H.D., and two years later the University of California at Los Angeles bestowed the degree of LL.D. at its fiftieth anniversary celebration.

These years also witnessed a continuation of Goodspeed's industry in publication. At the time of his retirement from the University in 1937, his friend and former student, S. V. McCasland, suggested that he translate the Apocrypha. This American translation appeared in 1938 and was followed one year later by *The Story of the Apocrypha*. During the next thirty years appeared such titles as *A History of Early Christian Literature* (1942), *Problems of New Testament Translation* (1945), *How to Read the Bible* (1946), *Paul* (1947), *A Life of Jesus* (1950), *The Twelve, the Story of Christ's Apostles* (1957) and finally, within three years of his death, *Matthew, Apostle and Evangelist* (1959).

As Edgar Goodspeed approached his ninetieth year, he was no longer able to leave his home except in rare instances, and on January 13, 1962, he died. Public ignorance of things biblical, which had so plagued him at the publication of his New Testament translation, and against which he had crusaded so diligently, pursued him to the end. The Associated Press obituary described him as having written "a condensed version of the Lord's Prayer" in *The New Testament, An American Translation*.[8]

From his earliest years Goodspeed had appeared to be destined by the process of acculturation for an ecclesiastical and academic career. The Baptist ministry was something of a tradition on both sides of his family, and he recalls that when he joined the Morgan Park Baptist Church his father was the minister and his mother the organist and director of the quartet. Moreover, "Grandfather was one of the deacons, and we boys felt identified with the church in the fullest sense of the word. And this sense of really belonging to the church we never lost."[9] Equally vivid and pleasant were childhood memories of camping out in the great attic to make room for the alumni and guests at the seminary commencement each May. "It had not dawned upon me, as I grew up in a theological seminary," Goodspeed writes, "that I

[8] *New York Times*, January 14, 1962, 84:2.
[9] *As I Remember*, 38.

would spend my active life in one, and its enveloping University. But so it was, and the friendship of those Seminary professors had great significance for me."[10] To inspire him further toward higher education was the example of his father, his older brother Charles, who went on to law school, and his cousins, George Goodspeed and James Ten Broeke, both of whom took the Ph.D. degree at Yale.

The man who was supremely influential in the educational development of Edgar Goodspeed, however, was William Rainey Harper. The former was a boy of eight when Harper joined the faculty of the Baptist Theological Union Seminary in Morgan Park. The memory of this teacher and friend was still vivid seventy years later:

> It was young Dr. Harper, whom I knew from my childhood, who created the unescapable impression, in a way he had, that I was going to study Hebrew with him and become a professor! I think my cousin George when he was tutoring us boys must have suggested to Dr. Harper that I had a linguistic bent; at any rate, by the time I was a junior in college it was understood that when I got through I was to go to Yale to study with Dr. Harper, which of course I did.[11]

All of Goodspeed's courses at Yale were with Harper, and when, after one year there, he transferred to the recently founded and newly opened University of Chicago, the close relationship continued. Harper had been called to be the University's first President.

Goodspeed's graduate studies remained on their Old Testament course until 1894–95 when a new direction was taken:

> It must have been after my second graduate year at Chicago that Dr. Burton one day called on me and suggested that I might be interested in transferring my studies to the New Testament field. I am sure he and the President must have talked of this change, for it would have been most unethical otherwise for him to suggest it. I was much attracted. I greatly admired Dr. Burton, and in teaching preparatory Greek through Homer for two or three years, on the side, I had come to feel attracted more to Greek than to Hebrew. Dr. Burton struck me as a remarkably acute and able scholar, as indeed he proved to be, in lexicography, syntax, and interpretation. So I took up New Testament Greek and interpretation, as my principal subject for my degree.[12]

Thus did Ernest D. Burton add his influence to the molding of Goodspeed as a scholar. Not long after the young student had joined his banner, Burton invited him to work on his Greek harmony of the Synoptic Gospels. Convinced that such a joint venture would teach him more about Burton's

[10] Ibid., 40.
[11] Ibid., 42.
[12] Ibid., 92.

methods than any amount of lectures, Goodspeed accepted. The undertaking extended over many years and left Goodspeed with the impression that in its preparation Burton had supplied the brains and he the brawn.

A new direction was also given to Goodspeed's studies when Burton brought Caspar Rene Gregory to the University for a single term in the summer of 1895. Gregory opened the whole world of manuscript study to Goodspeed. "So my change of department that year," he writes, "definitely shaped all the rest of my life."[13] Burton and Gregory thus played significant roles in the focusing of Goodspeed's interests within the limits of his general field of specialization. But to the time of his death, Harper remained the influence that shaped and fashioned the young scholar's remarkable preparation. It was Harper who appointed him to the University faculty but with the condition that he climax his six years of resident graduate work with a two-year visit to the German universities. And it was Harper, who in their last interview together said prophetically to Edgar Goodspeed, "Universities are made for fellows like you."[14]

[13] Ibid., 94.
[14] Ibid., 61.

II
EPHESIANS AND THE FORMATION
OF THE NEW TESTAMENT

The Letter to the Ephesians provides one of the most baffling chapters in the story of modern New Testament research. Although the date, destination and place of writing are naturally related questions, the essential problem is the question of authenticity. From the standpoint of chronology the debate on this question is relatively brief, for it was not until about the middle of the nineteenth century that one can speak of an Ephesian problem. By the second quarter of the twentieth century the debate over Ephesians had divided New Testament scholars into three groups: one maintaining its traditional authorship, a second holding it to be the work of a Paulinist, and a third contending that the unsolved problems on either side demanded an open verdict. It was at this juncture that Edgar Goodspeed entered the debate. Joining himself to the second group, he offered to the third a reconstruction designed to remove the factors which restrained the latter from a complete break with authenticity. Goodspeed was confident that the acceptance of his hypothesis would mark the end of 'the Ephesian problem.

The germ of what Goodspeed later developed into a major hypothesis first appeared as a passing allusion: "Ephesians was written in the latter part of the first century, not to any single church but as a general letter. It shows the influence of Colossians and must have been written in connection with the movement to collect Paul's letters, probably as an introduction to them."[1] The following year, the allusion became a chapter,[2] and in 1933 it reached book-length proportions.[3] In any examination of the hypothesis it is good to bear in mind the fact that Goodspeed never pretended to bring fresh data to the debate about the letter's authenticity. He took as his starting point

> a series of objective considerations generally accepted by modern learning, namely: that Ephesians is not by Paul; that it was not addressed to the Ephesians, but to Christians everywhere; that it comes from about 80–90 A.D. or a

---

[1] E. J. Goodspeed, *The Formation of the New Testament* (Chicago: University of Chicago Press, 1926) 28.

[2] E. J. Goodspeed, *New Solutions of New Testament Problems* (Chicago: University of Chicago Press, 1927) 11–20.

[3] E. J. Goodspeed, *The Meaning of Ephesians* (Chicago: University of Chicago Press, 1933).

little later; that it deals with Christian unity, against the rising sects; that it
shows acquaintance with other Pauline letters; and that it has certain ideas of
its own to bring forward and emphasize.[4]

The segment of New Testament scholarship which had accepted these con-
siderations was no more able to provide an occasion for the writing of Ephesians than were the Pauline defenders. Representative of those who found
this critical failure to be decisive for authenticity was Jülicher who climaxed
his discussion of the problem with the observation:

> Nor has a clear hypothesis of the circumstances under which a *Paulus re-*
> *divivus* might have composed the Epistle to the Ephesians ever been pro-
> vided, for it is impossible to see what purpose he could have served or why
> he made such a particularly thorough use of Colossians, when he himself did
> not lack independent ideas and was also acquainted with other Pauline
> Epistles.[5]

While others simply noted this gap, Goodspeed set himself to fill it. To his
mind the lack lay not in the adequacy of the facts at hand, but in their use.
Declaring his intention by printing Jülicher's challenge at the front of *The*
Meaning of Ephesians, he advanced just such a "clear hypothesis."[6]

The Goodspeed reconstruction presupposes a well-defined historical setting. The time is A.D. 80–90. Paul has passed from the scene and in the years
since his death has been all but forgotten. His letters, often composed swiftly
in the daily press of mission labors and intended to meet a specific need in
the time and place of their recipients, lie dusty in the church chests of his
scattered flocks. The Gospels of Mark and Matthew have been written but
betray no knowledge of Paul's letters. More significantly still, the author of
Luke-Acts, with his obvious interest in Paul, appears equally ignorant of this
rich primary source.

The theory now posits a Christian, probably an Asian, who is in close
relationship to the church at Colossae. In his possession is a copy of Paul's
letter to that congregation which he has read and reread until he almost
knows it by heart. Perhaps he is also familiar with the little letter to Philemon. These two documents are sufficient to make this man a Paulinist
through and through. One day there comes into his hands a copy of the

---

[4] E. J. Goodspeed, "The Place of Ephesians in the First Pauline Collection," *ATR* 12 (1929/
30) 192–93.

[5] A. Jülicher, *An Introduction to the New Testament* (trans. J. P. Ward; London: Smith,
Elder, & Co., 1904) 146–47.

[6] The hypothesis may be read in varying amount of detail in the following Goodspeed publications: *The Formation of the New Testament* (1926); *New Solutions of New Testament*
Problems (1927); *ATR* 12 (1929/30) 189–212; *The Meaning of Ephesians* (1933); *New Chap-*
ters in New Testament Study (1937); *An Introduction to the New Testament* (1937); *Chris-*
tianity Goes to Press (1940); *JBL* 64 (1945) 193–204; *Paul* (1947); *The Key to Ephesians* (1956).

recently published Acts. As the drama of the mission journeys unfolds before his mind's eye, a whole new dimension is added to his devotion to the man he had previously known only as a writer. It occurs to him that just as Paul wrote to the congregation at Colossae, so also he might have written letters to the congregations mentioned in the Acts. What a magnificent thing it would be if some of these letters had survived and could be assembled. It would be like Paul returning to the center of the Christian scene once more. The churches of the Acts are hopefully contacted, and with impressive results. Five different churches proved to have letters from Paul: Rome, Corinth, Philippi, Thessalonica and Galatia. His efforts have been richly rewarded, for he is the first man ever to read the collected letters of Paul! Having been stirred by Colossians alone, the spiritual heights and depths of the collection overwhelm him with the force of a revelation. Naturally, this treasure must be shared. The time is ripe, for the Acts has awakened the church at large to its massive indebtedness to Paul. But would Christians everywhere trouble to perceive the permanent riches so thoroughly intertwined with the apostolic word for specific situations long since past? What better guarantee could be devised than to preface the collection with a letter of introduction? Thus it was that this unknown Christian, fired by the inspiration of his master, unconsciously leaning most upon Colossians but drawing upon the riches of the entire corpus, weaving through his work the call to Christian unity needful for his day, composed the untitled covering letter of commendation destined to be misnamed in future years: The Letter to the Ephesians. Naturally, he put Paul's name at the head of it, for it was his intention that what he wrote should be Paul speaking through him. If he had put his own name to the document, he would have been properly branded as a plagiarist. Instead, he is the first Christian pseudepigrapher. In later statements of the hypothesis, Goodspeed yielded to the temptation to identify this unknown collector-author. He drew attention to the reflection of John Knox[7] that Paul's young protege and the bishop of Ephesus in Ignatius' day (A.D. 110–117) bore the name Onesimus. By assuming that these two are in fact the same person, Onesimus becomes both the collector of the Pauline corpus and the author of Ephesians. While conceding that this identification was in the realm of conjecture, Goodspeed claimed for it no small degree of probability.

Such, in brief, is Goodspeed's theory. In presenting it to the world of scholarship, he based his appeal for its acceptance on three points:

(1) It satisfies the very problems that from the first had vexed the critics of the letter. Here are the answers to the questions of why Ephesians is so Pauline without being Paul's; why Colossians is used so extensively amid the echoes of Paul's other letters; why a Paulinist would write the first Christian encyclical in the eighties; why the author chose to write in the name of

---

[7] *Philemon Among the Letters of Paul* (Chicago: University of Chicago Press, 1935) 54ff.

Paul; why Philemon was included in the collection; and why a non-Pauline
document was integral to the corpus from its day of publication.

(2) It illumines the meaning and significance of the letter, transforming
its former liabilities into assets. "It is the glory of historical interpretation,"
writes Goodspeed, "that when once the situation that called forth a document is determined, the document at once becomes luminous with
meaning."[8] Part I of *The Meaning of Ephesians* is an exposition of the letter
in the light of this hypothesis. For example, the first and second chapters of
Ephesians are viewed as a

> a summary of Pauline Christianity, in the form of a *Jubilate* over the
> blessedness of the Christian salvation . . . . It constitutes a glorious prelude to
> the Pauline letters. It is like the overture of an opera, foreshadowing the suc-
> cessive melodies that are to follow. All these great aspects of Christian truth
> and experience the reader was to find more fully dealt with in the letters
> themselves, of which this was simply the foretaste.[9]

The traditionally autobiographical and self-commendatory passages of
chapter 3 are interpreted as evidence of the introductory role of Ephesians.
The phrases, "as I have written briefly" (3:3) and "When you read this you
can perceive my insight into the mystery of Christ" (3:4), are taken as references to the accompanying corpus. As such, they are meant to portray a
significant side of Paul's activity unmentioned in the Acts. The readers are
informed that he was not only a missionary and a martyr. Here for the first
time Paul is introduced as a writer, whose works will edify the church. The
readers of Ephesians are expected to read the letters which follow and find
in them, as the writer himself had done, the proof of Paul's deep understanding of the mystery of Christ.

Even such apparently simple passages as Eph 6:1-4 are said to give up
new significance when read in the light of this hypothesis. Goodspeed judges
that the man who treated the duties of fatherhood so barrenly as the author
of Col 3:21 could never have written Eph 6:4 with its addition: "but bring
them up in the discipline and instruction of the Lord." This passage points
to an age when Paul's vivid and immediate apocalyptic had waned, to a
time when the church had begun to see that its future depended in no small
measure upon its children. In short, this seemingly commonplace verse in
Ephesians is taken to be the first sign of Christian education in the home.

Goodspeed felt that results like these were self-authenticating for his
theory. The many matters that had to be suppressed or ignored on the assumption of Pauline authorship now blossomed into full significance. On this
basis he concludes: "The test to which we have subjected the theory advanced as to the origin of the epistle is fully met; the theory illumines the

---

[8] *The Meaning of Ephesians*, 14.
[9] Ibid., 20–21.

whole letter, and offers a definite situation for its composition which throws
a convincing light upon page after page."[10]

(3) It is substantiated by a tabular exhibit of the relationship of Ephesians to the nine letters generally recognized as being from Paul. This parallel column presentation resembles a Gospel harmony in format and constitutes Part II of *The Meaning of Ephesians*. The first column contains the
continuous text of Ephesians broken into short lines to show its resemblance
to the text of Colossians as well as to the other Pauline letters. The parallel
parts of Colossians are printed in the second column, and those of the re-
maining letters in columns three and four. The claim is made that "every
one of the nine letters, even 2 Thessalonians and Philemon, is convincingly
reflected in Ephesians."[11] Since Paul would hardly have limited himself to
those nine letters which were to be preserved to the church, Goodspeed
argues, the most natural and probable explanation is that the writer of
Ephesians has found and assembled those letters and has undertaken to
introduce them to the Christian world.

The implications of Goodspeed's Ephesian contribution reach backward
to the Pauline corpus and forward to the later Christian literature. The first
part of this statement is already apparent. As the Ephesians theory unfolds,
it becomes increasingly clear that it is integrally related to a theory concerning the Pauline letter collection. No one was more aware of this fact than
Goodspeed himself: "The problem of Ephesians is inextricably intertwined
with that of the Pauline corpus; it cannot be dealt with apart from it."[12]
Once Goodspeed committed himself to the position that Ephesians was specifically written as an introduction to the Pauline corpus, the creation of that
corpus had to be explained. Up to this time, students of the problem were
generally agreed that from the first Paul's letters had been highly valued by
the recipient congregations,[13] and that there had been an early exchange of
letters among them.[14] As has been noted, Goodspeed suggested that the situation was quite the opposite. The idea that Paul's letters must have circulated early because they were so prized he set aside as a modern attitude
transferred to antiquity. Modern readers make this judgment of Paul's letters because they know them in all the prestige, familiarity and authority of
their present form and place in a New Testament. Their original reception
was not so impressive. Once read and heeded, an individual letter would
have fulfilled its purpose and, like the vast majority of letters, would sink
into obscurity or oblivion. That the churches would not treasure them, let
alone circulate them, is understandable because letters like Galatians,

[10] Ibid., 73.
[11] Ibid., 80.
[12] *The Meaning of Ephesians*, 9.
[13] A. von Harnack, *Die Briefsammlung des Apostels Paulus* (Leipzig: J. C. Hinrichs, 1926) 7.
[14] K. Lake, *The Earlier Epistles of Paul* (London: Rivingtons, 1911) 366.

2 Thessalonians, and 1 Corinthians were not very pleasant reading for their original recipients. That the churches *did* not treasure them is apparent for two reasons. First, there is no record of Paul's letters being read in public worship until about 180, almost a century after they had been collected and published. If the collection could be so long ignored, how much more the individual letters scattered among the churches![15] Second, had the letters been early prized and circulated, they would certainly have been utilized by the authors of Mark, Matthew, and Luke-Acts.

Shortly after the appearance of Luke-Acts, however, the situation is completely reversed. Suddenly, every Christian document—the Revelation, Hebrews, 1 Clement, 1 Peter, the letters of Ignatius and Polycarp, the Gospel of John—shows acquaintance with Paul's letters. Nor is this acquaintance limited to one or two of the letters; it spans the entire corpus.[16] What could have worked this remarkable transformation, asks Goodspeed, but the publication of the Pauline corpus? And what could have motivated that momentous event but the appearance of Luke-Acts? This means that the *terminus a quo* for the Pauline corpus is the date of the Acts. For reasons to be noticed later, the writing of the Revelation is taken as its *terminus ad quem*.

Having suggested to this point an occasion and date for the collection as well as an identity for the collector, Goodspeed was well on the way toward a complete theory on the Pauline corpus. All that was necessary to round it out were views concerning its birthplace, original size and sequence.

From his first mention of the corpus problem, Goodspeed was convinced that Ephesus had given Paul's collected letters to the world:

> In writing to the Ephesians about 107, Ignatius says that Paul in every letter remembers or recalls them—a remark of some difficulty, since some of Paul's best-known letters say nothing about Ephesus. What Ignatius probably means is that in view of the Ephesians' connection with the publication of Paul's letters, every such letter brings them to the readers' mind. Certainly almost everything points to Ephesus as the place of origin of the collection.[17]

What that "everything" consisted of is spelled out more fully in Goodspeed's later emphasis on the role of early Christian publication in the rise of New Testament literature.[18] He believed that this role is commonly neglected because the matter is obscured in the public mind by the confusion between publication and printing. The latter belongs to modern times, but publication flourished in antiquity. It is not surprising that the first steps in Christian

---

[15] E. J. Goodspeed, "The Editio Princeps of Paul," *JBL* 64 (1945) 201.

[16] E. J. Goodspeed, *An Introduction to the New Testament* (Chicago: University of Chicago Press, 1937) 211, 214.

[17] *The Formation of the New Testament*, 28–29.

[18] See especially, *New Chapters in New Testament Study* (New York: The Macmillan Company, 1937) 1–49; and *Christianity Goes to Press* (New York: The Macmillan Company, 1940) 26–78.

publication took place in Rome where the religious needs of that congregation called forth the writing of Mark. Another forward step was taken at Antioch with the publication of Matthew. But not until a little after 90 was the church to find its publishing center with the production of Luke-Acts at Ephesus.[19] By this assertion, the Pauline corpus becomes but one important part of a flood of Christian literature which flowed from Ephesus. The flow began when the first three of Paul's four known letters to Corinth were "in all probability" written there. It continued with the writing of Luke-Acts and reached flood stage with the assembling of the Pauline corpus, the writing of Ephesians, the Revelation, the Fourth Gospel and the publication of the Ignatian and Johannine letters. It was climaxed by the making there of a fourfold Gospel corpus.[20]

Goodspeed's first reference to the size of the collection suggested that in its earliest form it probably contained seven letters to churches.[21] A year later, however, he was prepared to offer a different and somewhat more detailed description.[22] On the basis of evidence gathered from the reflections of the collection in the letters of Clement, Ignatius, and Polycarp, and from Ephesians itself, he is confident that after the introductory encyclical—our Ephesians—"the original collection included at least eight letters, addressed to six churches. This is almost exactly the list adopted by Marcion, about 140, except that he included Philemon and called Ephesians 'Laodiceans', which would give a total of ten letters, to seven churches and one individual." The idea that the original collection was limited to letters to seven churches was one that Goodspeed was prepared to defend.[23] He noted that fondness for the number seven pervades the earliest gospel as well as Luke-Acts. This same interest is intensified in the Revelation which was written under the shadow of Ephesus in the very days that witnessed the collection and publication of the corpus. Thus, he argued, it is certainly not inconceivable nor even improbable that the collectors of Paul's letters might have felt an interest in building their collection up to seven. This point, when added to a suggestion about the destiny of the missing Laodicean letter, becomes a factor in Goodspeed's solution to such problems as: (1) What has become of the "letter from Laodicea" mentioned in Col 4:16? (2) How did a personal

---

[19] Goodspeed writes: "The place of origin of Luke-Acts is a matter of much debate among scholars, but I cannot doubt that it was written in Ephesus, which would mean that its writer was at the time at any rate an Ephesian and was writing primarily for Ephesian readers. Consider first, the amount of space devoted in his second volume, the Acts, to Ephesus. Luke gives Ephesus more space than any other Greek church receives, and further, Paul's only extended farewell to any of his churches is the one to the elders of Ephesus. This would be a strange proceeding in a work written in Rome or Corinth" (*New Chapters in New Testament Study*, 27).

[20] Ibid., 39ff.

[21] *The Formation of the New Testament*, 27

[22] *New Solutions of New Testament Problems*, 50ff.

[23] "Ephesians in the Pauline Collection," *ATR* 12 (1929/30) 199–200.

letter like Philemon come to have a place in a collection of church letters?
(3) How does there happen to be a "Laodiceans" in the Marcion corpus, the
earliest extant list of Paul's letters? (4) How did the introductory encyclical
come to be called Ephesians? The key to this intricate reconstruction is the
conjecture that the present Philemon is the "letter from Laodicea." Once
that is granted, the theory continues as follows: The original collection consisted of the nameless introductory encyclical (the modern Ephesians) and
letters to the churches at Colossae, Corinth, Galatia, Philippi, Rome, Thessalonica and Laodicea (the modern Philemon). Although it is common to regard Philemon as a letter to an individual, it is actually addressed to "Philemon our beloved fellow worker and Apphia our sister and Archippus our
fellow soldier and the church in your house." It is thus, in form, another
church letter.[24] That the church addressed was at Laodicea is suggested by
Col 4:16f: "And when this letter has been read among you, have it read also
in the church of the Laodiceans; and see that you read also the letter from
Laodicea. And say to Archippus, 'See that you fulfill the ministry which you
have received in the Lord.'" If this indicates (as Goodspeed holds) that
Archippus was at Laodicea, then the letter to Philemon was sent to that
place. This explains why Philemon was included in a collection limited to
church letters, and raises the question of how it received its present name.
At this point attention is called to the hard things said about the Laodicean
church in the Revelation (3:15ff.). As this congregation came into increasing
dishonor, its name was dropped from the honored roll of the corpus, and the
name of Philemon, the first person mentioned in the Laodicean letter, was
substituted. This action reduced the number of churches named to six. Reverence for the number seven then created a desire that a church name be
given to the nameless introductory encyclical. Marcion's list apparently reflects a stage in the development when the seventh letter had become Philemon, but the substitution was not established. Influenced by the lingering
tradition that the collection had contained a letter to Laodicea, he mistaken-
ly assumed it to be the encyclical. Subsequently, the encyclical received the
honored name of its place of origin and the words ἐν Ἐφέσῳ gained en-
trance to its text.

It was inevitable that Goodspeed's Ephesian theory would also lead him
into the problem of the sequence of the original corpus. If Ephesians was
composed as an introduction to the corpus it would naturally appear at its
head. An immediate difficulty for the theory lay in the fact that there is no
evidence to substantiate this position for Ephesians. Marcion's list begins
with Galatians; the Muratorian list begins with Corinthians, followed by
Ephesians. Goodspeed's initial effort to overcome this difficulty involved

[24] A. von Harnack had also made this suggestion: "Die Rezeption des Philemonbriefs beweist
nicht, dass man über den Kreis der Gemeindebriefe hinausgegangen ist; denn auch er ist an
eine 'Ekklesia' gerichtet" (*Die Briefsammlung des Apostels Paulus*, 10).

giving preference to the Muratorian list and then making Corinthian editors of a second edition of the corpus (when 2 Corinthians was added) responsible for its order.[25] Later, both aspects of this solution were abandoned in favor of the case for the priority of Ephesians advanced by John Knox.[26] Knox accepted Marcion's list as being nearest to the original, noting that it appears to be based on an order of decreasing length. According to the traditional stichometry of the New Testament as deduced by J. Rendel Harris,[27] a strict order of the letters by decreasing length would be this:

>Corinthians (1 and 2)
>Romans
>Ephesians
>Thessalonians (1 and 2)
>Galatians
>Colossians
>Philippians
>Philemon

Marcion's order was this:

>Galatians
>Corinthians (1 and 2)
>Romans
>Thessalonians (1 and 2)
>Laodiceans (Ephesians)
>Colossians
>Philippians
>Philemon

A comparison of the strict order by length with Marcion's list will show that after Galatians (which Marcion presumably placed first as his favorite) Marcion deviates at just one point: Ephesians follows Thessalonians when it should precede it. Knox offers this explanation for the variation:

>May it not be that Ephesians follows Thessalonians because it takes the place, left vacant, so to speak, by Marcion's putting of Galatians in first position, the position which Ephesians itself previously occupied. If the original list was strictly in order of length, it began with Corinthians, and Ephesians preceded, and Galatians followed, Thessalonians. But in that case, why should Marcion's lifting of Galatians out of its place disturb the position of Ephesians? If, however, Ephesians headed the first list and Marcion merely transposed it and

[25] *The Formation of the New Testament*, 29ff.
[26] *Philemon Among the Letters of Paul*, 38ff.
[27] "Stichometry," *American Journal of Philology* 4 (1883) 317.

Galatians, the position of Ephesians in Marcion's canon is naturally accounted for.[28]

This demonstration was embraced by Goodspeed as the confirmation of his position that Ephesians stood first in the corpus.[29]

Turning now to the second part of the initial summary statement,[30] it is necessary to trace the implications of Goodspeed's Ephesian theory forward to the subsequent Christian literature.

According to the theory, the composition of Ephesians and the making of the Pauline corpus bear the same date. Since the publication of Luke-Acts about 90 provided the motivation for both projects, it is obvious why the date of Luke-Acts becomes their *terminus a quo*. It may be less apparent why the appearance of the Revelation about 95 is regarded as their *terminus ad quem*. The answer lies in Goodspeed's conviction that "the collection of Paul's letters was as important and influential an event in the growth of the New Testament as the writing of almost any book in it."[31] From 90–110 this Pauline collection is seen as the dominating influence in Christian literature. The first document to reflect that influence is the Revelation. Goodspeed suggests that New Testament scholarship has overlooked the strangest feature of this book: the fact that it begins with a corpus of letters to churches.[32] This feature sets the Revelation apart from all Jewish and Christian apocalypses and demands an explanation. This is particularly so since its corpus is not a real collection of scattered letters but an artificial literary creation, *de novo*, used to preface an entirely different type of literature. The only explanation of this phenomenon is that the author of the Revelation was not only exposed to a collection of Christian letters but moreover was so impressed by it that he swerved from his own literary style and began his apocalypse with letters. Cited as evidence of this position is the use of Paul's unique epistolary salutation, χάρις ὑμῖν καὶ εἰρήνη, and the arrangement of one general letter (paralleling Ephesians) followed by letters to seven churches (paralleling the corpus).

In addition to the Revelation, the use of letters of considerable length for Christian instruction suddenly became general. The Letter to the Hebrews is so suggestive of Paul that the ancients who did not think he wrote it himself attributed it to one of his followers. Goodspeed agrees with the latter view but suggests that the Pauline influence was literary rather than personal. In 1 Peter, the church at Rome begins to do that work of instructing churches it was challenged to do by the Letter to the Hebrews. But what had suggested the letter method? What but the collection of Paul? 1 Clement is

[28] Knox, *Philemon Among the Letters of Paul*, 41f.

[29] Goodspeed, *An Introduction to the New Testament*, 226.

[30] Ibid., 55.

[31] *Christianity Goes to Press* (New York: The Macmillan Company, 1940) 55.

[32] *New Solutions of New Testament Problems*, 21ff.

regarded as the work of a mediocre man who is straining after his great models in the corpus. The letters of John reflect the corpus in miniature, being composed of a general letter (paralleling Ephesians), a church letter (paralleling Paul's church letters), and an individual letter (paralleling Philemon). In some manner, the influence of Ephesians and its Pauline corpus is detected in Ignatius, Polycarp, Timothy, Titus, James, Jude, 2 Peter, Barnabas, the Epistle of the Apostles, and the Martyrdom of Polycarp. The collecting of the Johannine and Ignatian Epistles, the Pastoral and Catholic Epistles, and the four Gospels is laid to the same influence. As Goodspeed himself observes upon surveying the sweep of his literary theory: "the thing really becomes an avalanche."

The appeal of Goodspeed's Ephesian hypothesis was severely limited from the outset. It was addressed primarily to those who were already convinced by the arguments against the Pauline authorship. The point of this restriction was not lost on Goodspeed's chief supporter: "To those, however, who are not already persuaded by them, and feel no necessity of looking for some alternative to Pauline authorship, this theory has little to offer. Indeed it may appear little more than 'a tissue of improbabilities.'"[33] It is fair to say that this limitation remains in force today. Writers on Ephesians for whom the question of authorship is answered by the letter itself either refute the theory or simply ignore it. Without a doubt, Goodspeed expected this reaction from those within the traditional position. It is very doubtful, however, that he anticipated so limited an acceptance among the scholars who denied the authenticity of this letter. To them he came, offering solutions for all their unsolved problems. American and British critics, however, greeted the hypothesis with caution, and even those who found it attractive embraced it with definite reservations or modifications. German scholarship, which had contributed so much to Goodspeed's key assumption of unauthenticity, never took his efforts seriously.

Perhaps a cautious response was inevitable, for the reconstruction is entirely too literary. Everything is made to depend on books. In literary criticism, writes H. J. Cadbury, "we take the books we have and try to arrange them into a series of cause and effect, as though books were more precipitated by books than by other and living factors in the environment, and more by books preserved to our times than by books that have been lost."[34] Thus, at almost every point, Goodspeed's hypothesis encountered demands for solid evidence—evidence that it was unable to supply. Too frequently the arguments offered to substantiate such points as the thirty-year neglect of Paul and his letters, the role of Luke-Acts in Paul's supposed

---

[33] C. L. Mitton, *The Epistle to the Ephesians* (Oxford: Clarendon Press, 1951) 45.

[34] "The Dilemma of Ephesians," *NTS* 5 (1958/59) 92. He adds: "This theory of literary precipitation leading to a kind of chain reaction is characteristic of E. J. Goodspeed and his pupils, as in their views on Ephesians . . . " (92n).

revival, the character and purpose of Ephesians, its priority in the original corpus, and the decisive influence of the corpus on the formation of the New Testament, fell short of being convincing. The appeal of the Goodspeed theory has always resided in its ingenious ability to provide an answer to every troublesome question raised by Ephesians. But it cannot overcome the doubt inherent in a method which constructs an historical situation out of unsolved difficulties and then offers it as their solution.

Overshadowing these myriad weaknesses, however, is the decisive question of authenticity. The ongoing debate over Pauline authorship is of the greatest significance for the hypothesis, for here it is always face to face with potential annihilation. This vulnerability was built into the theory by Goodspeed's conviction that the unauthenticity of Ephesians was a position already won. This question, regarded by many as one of the insolubles of New Testament research, he took as a firm foundation upon which to build. The kindliest judgment possible of this decision would be that it is overly optimistic. In the very years that Goodspeed was developing his position, Harnack was asking whether the collector of the Pauline corpus was so injudicious in his task that he took the unauthentic for the authentic.[35] Aware that the question is particularly relevant for Ephesians, he points out that the great age of the corpus makes it most unlikely that one of the letters could be a forgery. This view rests not upon the notion that false letters were not circulating so early but rather upon the conviction that such forgeries would not be accepted by the primitive congregations without contradiction.

The same reluctance on the part of Goodspeed to allow any powers of discrimination to the first-century Christians appears at another place. In each presentation of the hypothesis he insists that Paul did not write letters with publication in mind, much less anticipate or share in their eventual collection. The point is well taken. But in the interpretation of the personal allusions in Eph 3, the author of those passages obviously represents Paul as the one who has collected his letters and is now introducing and commending them to his readers! Would these Christian readers in the eighties, knowing that Paul had died some twenty-five years previously, have no hesitancy about accepting a document in which he was now introducing them to his own letter collection?

It is precisely the uncertainties in all such attempts to probe the thought patterns of other centuries that have always made an impressive number of scholars hesitant about denying Ephesians or Paul. If it is difficult to determine the ancients' views on authenticity or to recreate the criteria by which a document might be accepted or rejected, how much more baffling are the problems of the historical psychology of individual authorship? Selecting arbitrary proportions, Cadbury asks: "Which is more likely—that an imitator of Paul in the first century composed a writing ninety or ninety-five per

---

[35] *Die Briefsammlung des Apostels Paulus*, 11f.

cent in accordance with Paul's style or that Paul himself wrote a letter diverging five or ten per cent from his usual style?"[36] Writing in much the same vein, H. Chadwick concludes:

> Ultimately, the discussion turns on the bottomless problem: What manner of man was the apostle? If we begin from the conventional portrait, it is not easy to suppose Eph. to be Pauline. But the Procrustean picture may be mistaken. We have no sufficient ground for regarding him as a man incapable of producing Eph., and in any event the argument against the tradition, strong as it may be, falls some distance short of the demonstration claimed for it by the overenthusiastic.[37]

And Markus Barth introduces four minor arguments against pseudonymity and in favor of authenticity with the words, "In view of the insufficient linguistic and historical arguments, and of the prejudicial character of the theological reasons exhibited against Ephesians, it is advisable for the time being to still consider Paul its author."[38] It was Goodspeed's hope that with the appearance of his theory, the scholarly impasse on Ephesians would be broken. Today, the realization of that hope seems farther off than ever, for every judicious opinion rendered in favor of the authenticity of Ephesians or in favor of keeping the question open thereby weighs against Goodspeed's elaborate hypothesis.

[36] *The Dilemma of Ephesians*, 92.

[37] *Peake's Commentary on the Bible* (ed. M. Black and H. H. Rowley; London: Thomas Nelson and Sons, 1962) 982.

[38] *Ephesians* (Garden City, N.Y.: Doubleday & Company, 1974) 49.

III
THE NEW TESTAMENT:
AN AMERICAN TRANSLATION

On February 24, 1920, Goodspeed read a paper on modern speech translations before the New Testament Club at the University of Chicago. The paper discussed the three leading private translations of the day, Twentieth Century, Weymouth, and Moffatt, and criticized them freely. In the discussion that followed the presentation, Shirley Jackson Case suggested to Goodspeed that if he saw so many flaws in these versions, perhaps he should do one himself. Goodspeed recalled that this remark evoked some laughter at his expense. Not everyone, however, took the remark as humor. A representative of the Chicago University Press who was present brought the idea to his editor. The latter invited Goodspeed to undertake the project for the University Press. His response was to try his hand at the Gospel of Mark. That spring, whenever asked to speak in the Divinity Chapel, he would simply read a few pages from his new translation. The attention and interest accorded these readings, together with the encouragement received from similar readings in family gatherings, resulted in the decision to go on with the project. The translation was in preparation for three years during which time Goodspeed was also occupied with teaching in the New Testament department and serving as Secretary to the President of the University. "I spent the day in the office," he recalls, "and as my oculist had long before forbidden me to do any close work at night, my time for the translation was very limited."[1] It became his practice to do no more than fifteen or sixteen verses at a session. The last of the manuscript of the translation was turned in to the Press during the last week of May, 1923, and publication took place in October.

From the preface to the translation and from subsequent publications it is possible to trace Goodspeed's motivation for setting forth a new translation. As the makers of the Revised Version (1881) had done before him,[2] he emphasized the very significant progress made in the area of the Greek text

---

[1] E. J. Goodspeed, *As I Remember* (New York: Harper & Brothers, 1953) 162.

[2] "Their [the translators of 1611] chief guides appear to have been the later editions of Stephanus and of Beza, and also, to a certain extent, the Complutensian Polyglott. All these were founded for the most part on manuscripts of late date, few in number, and used with little critical skill" (Preface to the Revised Version, 1881).

since 1611. "Within twenty years after the publication of the King James
Version," he wrote, "there appeared in England the first of those ancient
manuscripts of the Greek Testament which have in the past three centuries
transformed our knowledge of its text."[3] With unmistakable enthusiasm
Goodspeed relates the story of the great manuscript discoveries of the nineteenth century. The result of these remarkable developments for the modern
translator is the knowledge that "he has a much more ancient and trust-
worthy Greek text to translate than the scholars of King James."[4] Goodspeed
had no criticism of the textual improvements made by the revisers of 1881,
but he deplored the fact that they limited themselves to that particular type
of improvement. That revision

> was largely a textual matter, for no one even thought of modernizing the
> phraseology. It was the new found manuscript material reflected in new
> critical texts, Tischendorf and Tregelles, that had made revision inevi-
> table . . . . The strongly conservative attitude of the time to any moderniza-
> tion of Biblical language is revealed in the second of the principles of
> revision adopted by the sponsors of the undertaking . . . (namely) to limit
> their alterations as far as possible to the language of the King James and
> earlier versions. This necessarily made their English more antique than that
> of the version they were revising.[5]

Nothing horrified Goodspeed more, however, than the popular notion
that the modern Bible translator merely tinkers with the King James Version, replacing its archaic words with their modern equivalents. For him, the
case for new translation rested partly upon the progress in the knowledge of
Greek gained through the method of comparative philology, partly upon the
twentieth-century advances in New Testament lexicography, but chiefly
upon the papyrus discoveries of the late nineteenth and early twentieth
centuries. He was convinced that the latter rendered intolerable not simply
the individual words but the entire linguistic style of the King James Version
and its revisions. The papyri solved the problem of what kind of Greek was
in the New Testament. It was not the classical or literary Greek of its own
day nor the "biblical" Greek of the Septuagint. The papyri showed that the
New Testament was written in the vernacular Greek of its time, the language of everyday life. This discovery set Goodspeed solidly on the side of
the modern speech translations which he described in these words:

> The realization that revision was not enough, that the New Testament must
> be retranslated if it is to reach the modern reader with anything like the

[3] *The Making of the English New Testament* (Chicago: University of Chicago Press, 1925)
52.
    [4] E. J. Goodspeed, *Problems of New Testament Translation* (Chicago: University of
Chicago Press, 1945) 4.
    [5] *New Chapters in New Testament Study* (New York: Macmillan, 1937) 87.

force it had in antiquity, marks all these recent efforts, as does the consciousness that the only appropriate vehicle for such retranslation is the common
vernacular English of everyday life.[6]

In one sense Goodspeed was a latecomer to the modern speech movement, for in 1855 Andrews Norton had published in Boston *The Gospels, a
new translation*, in which he employed a contemporary idiom. Three years
later, in the same city, Leicester Ambrose Sawyer issued the entire New
Testament under the title, *The New Testament, translated from the original Greek with chronological arrangement of books*. Although these two
versions are little known, they mark the beginning of the long line of present versions which use current English as the medium of expression.[7] Mention has been made of Goodspeed's familiarity with the well-known trio of
modern speech versions, *The Twentieth Century New Testament* (1904),
The New Testament in Modern Speech by Richard F. Weymouth (1903),
and *The New Testament, A New Translation* by James Moffatt (1913).
Although he reports that he criticized them freely before the New Testament Club at the University of Chicago, very little specific criticism of them
appears in his various publications. He described the Twentieth Century as
"one of the best of the modern speech versions"[8] and felt that its "combination of sound learning and freedom of expression made its appearance a
notable event in the history of modern translations."[9] He judged Weymouth's translation much less informal than its title ("an idiomatic translation into everyday English") suggests[10] and deplored the amount of space the
publishers had given to footnotes in early editions.[11] Nevertheless, he followed Weymouth in the full modern paragraphing of his translation. From
the beginning, he wrote, "my translation was geared to public reading, a
course so different from Dr. Moffatt's."[12] With the exception of these minor
criticisms, then, Goodspeed appears to have had genuine admiration for the
efforts of his predecessors. Yet because they were all British, he believed that
the need for a specifically American translation remained. "I felt," he recalls,
"as Chaplain Ballentine had felt before me, that American popular usage is
so different from British that there was room for a version in a definitely
American idiom, and offered an American translation."[13] To illustrate the

---

[6] *The Making of the English New Testament*, 110.

[7] Hugh Pope, *English Versions of the Bible* (St. Louis: B. Herder Book Co., 1952) 546.

[8] *New Chapters in New Testament Study*, 98.

[9] *The Making of the English New Testament*, 107.

[10] Ibid., 109.

[11] *As I Remember*, 160.

[12] Ibid., 158.

[13] E. J. Goodspeed, "The Present State of Bible Translation," *JBR* 18 (1950) 100. The refer-
ence is apparently to Frank Schell Ballentine who published between 1899–1901 *The Modern
American Bible* in five volumes. Despite its title, *The Modern American Bible*, only the New
Testament was ever published. After emphasizing the changes in the English language from the

American-English differences, Goodspeed settled on two examples which he used whenever he discussed the issue. One concerned the British way of speaking of wheat as "corn," a term which means something so different in this country:

> This may seem an insignificant point, but as a matter of fact it reduces the familiar story of the apostles finding a path through a field of standing wheat to a positive absurdity; picture them plucking ears of corn—no easy task!— husking them, which requires a good deal of exertion, and then of all things eating the kernels! If it was dry enough to shell, it was too dry to eat! Of course what we call "corn" was unknown in Palestine in Jesus' day, and it is planted in rows, or hills, not sown broadcast. The disciples were simply push-ing their way, as they had a perfect right to do, along a familiar path now overgrown with the broadcast wheat, and as they went they unconsciously rubbed a few kernels free of the chaff and munched them. An American reader would never get this picture from the King James or any British trans-lation. He would miss the point of the story, which is that the slight, perhaps unconscious act of rubbing three or four grains free of their tiny husks would be to the Pharisees' way of thinking, threshing, and hence working, on the Sabbath day![14]

The other example concerned monetary references. "Why should we forever seek to impose the sterling currency upon the New Testament—pounds, shillings, pence and farthings?" he demanded:

> That currency has no more to do with the world of Jesus and the apostles than dollars and cents have. Yet some earnest people will declare that to speak of dollars and cents in the New Testament in an 'anachronism' all unconscious that pounds, shillings, pence and farthings are equally anachro-nistic there. If the purpose of New Testament translation is to bring what the New Testament writers meant to convey directly and vividly before the modern American reader, then it should not be necessary for him to detour through a course in sixteenth century English, such as is necessary for the understanding of even the simpler parts of the New Testament. There are more readers of the English Bible in America than in any other country in the world, and there is room for a translation made in their own vernacular.[15]

It was Goodspeed's goal to supply this American translation.

---

seventeenth to the twentieth centuries, he wrote: "If this is true in successive centuries in the same country, it is equally true of different countries with the same tongue in the same century. The American use of words differs largely from the English. So it will hardly be denied that spellings and meanings that are foreign to us and make the Bible harder to understand in America, ought to be replaced by spellings and words that are usual and clear with us," *The Modern American Bible* (New York: Thomas Whittaker, 1901) V, 12.

[14] *As I Remember*, 159.

[15] *New Chapters in New Testament Study*, 113.

He set out to achieve this goal with an awareness of the myriad difficulties of New Testament translation. At the same time, he was convinced that most of these difficulties could be overcome by the skill of the translator, first in relation to the Greek original, and second, in relation to the English rendering. Two years after his translation appeared he published *The Making of the English New Testament.*[16] In its final chapter he pointed out how the text, equipment, and attitude of the modern student combine to place him in a very advantageous position to translate the New Testament. Then, in 1945, he brought out a book whose overall aim was "to introduce the reader into a translator's workshop and to show him the tools and materials with which the translator works."[17] These tools and materials constitute all the aids learning can provide—translations, commentaries, grammars, lexicons, concordances, papyri, inscriptions, monographs, articles—everything one can reach that bears on the primary goal: to find out just what each of the New Testament writers meant each sentence to convey. That he was unusually qualified to handle these tools and materials, Goodspeed did not doubt:

> My first serious acquaintance with the Greek New Testament began in 1887 in sophomore year in college—I was not quite sixteen—when Professor Richard S. Colwell had us provide ourselves with a convenient student's edition of the Westcott and Hort text, then comparatively new; it had come out only six years before. We read the Gospel of John, in reasonable installments, for our Monday recitation, and I became so taken with the work that I continued it by myself at odd hours or moments so that before I was graduated at eighteen I had read the New Testament through in Greek, though of course in a most careless fashion. So the translating of it was an old practice of mine. And of course in my graduate work I had pursued it critically and made something of a specialty of its syntax and lexicography. My work on papyri also now came into focus with my New Testament studies and proved of great assistance, as did my Greek indexes of the Apostolic Fathers and the early apologists, published at Leipzig in 1907, 1912. Greek syntax studies with Dr. Burton and Dr. William Gardner Hale fortified me on that side. I had taught elementary Greek, Xenophon and Homer for a number of years, and for twenty years had taught reading the Greek New Testament and New Testament grammar every year at least once, on the University level. All this was to prove of the utmost value to me in this new undertaking. I recite it all here, because my preparation was soon to be vigorously called into question, in every part of the country and overseas.[18]

Impressive as this personal equipment was, Goodspeed did not claim it to be superior to the combined skills of the English and American committees

---

[16] (Chicago: University of Chicago Press, 1925).
[17] *Problems of New Testament Translation,* 1ff.
[18] *As I Remember,* 160–61.

on revision. The weakness of their work lay not in their Greek scholarship but in their English rendering. Once the translator had discovered what each New Testament writer meant each sentence to convey, he then should set himself "to cast that thought in such English as the translator would have used if he had thought of it himself."[19] Indeed,

> the best translation is not one that keeps forever before the reader's mind the fact that this is a translation, not an original English composition, but one that makes him feel that he is looking into the ancient writer's mind, as he would into that of a contemporary. This is, indeed, no light matter to execute, but it is, nevertheless, the task of any serious translator.[20]

The faults of the first English versions stemmed from their failure to recognize and follow this principle. Their adoption of a word for word method, with never a glance at the line of thought proved to be the bane of the English Bible from Tyndale to the revised versions. It would be difficult to overstate the emphasis Goodspeed placed on the English style of a translator. While acknowledging that sound learning is his most fundamental consideration, he insisted that good taste in English expression is almost equally important. He gratefully recalled the memory of William Gardner Hale who would urge his students to cultivate their English feeling. Goodspeed's aim, then, was to avoid translation English which he regarded as almost no English at all, to exclude all echoes of the familiar "Bible English" of the older versions, and in their place to use American idiom. Lest anyone conclude that this is a simple matter, he revealed the secret of his own method:

> It is often assumed that the familiar style, the style of modern speech, is an easy, careless style to write. Quite the opposite. True, it is not learned in the study or in the classroom, but in social contact with well-bred men and women who can talk. There is a kind of churchman and a kind of scholar that has no general social contacts; and such men do not learn the familiar style, and consequently cannot write it. They may think themselves above it, but the result is the same. When they try to write it, they lapse into all sorts of barbarisms. To point some of these out would be ungenerous. It is simple enough to write the stiff formal style of the old translators, but it is far more taxing to write in the familiar spoken English of today. We must remember Hale's old maxim, "Cultivate your English feeling!" Many present-day translators would not even see what he meant![21]

Goodspeed felt that a strict application of his principles to the Greek original and the English rendering would produce a version with four distinct qualities. It would be objective, readable, interpretive and contemporary. He

---

[19] *Problems of New Testament Translation*, 2.
[20] Ibid., 8.
[21] *As I Remember*, 163.

believed the time had come when the modern New Testament student could see, as former centuries did not, that the task of the translator is to express the meaning of the individual writer he is translating with all the clearness and candor of which the translator is capable, whether he himself agrees with it or not. Any other method would simply force the ancient writer to agree with the translator. The modern translator must pursue the ancient writer's meaning with the same detachment with which the chemist looks at his test tube or the biologist looks through his microscope. His aim is not to buttress a theology but to find out what each New Testament writer had to tell.[22] And in order to be faithful to the New Testament itself the translation would be readable. "The Greek Christian of the second century," said Goodspeed, "had no more readable books in his world than the gospels and Acts."[23] Therefore a translation which was faithful in its individual parts but unfaithful in its total impression would be wrong in principle. That had been the greatest weakness of earlier translators. They had been more concerned with words than with phrases, with clauses than with sentences, with verses than with paragraphs. The test of a translation, like the test of a book, "is not a line here and there, but coherence, movement, action; not how easily we may pull it to pieces, and what interesting pieces it makes, but how it first interests us, then absorbs us, and finally sweeps us along."[24] Moreover, Goodspeed contended that where the original language was ambiguous the good translator would shield this from the reader by becoming an interpreter. The translator cannot escape the many things the commentator can evade. Rather, as Moffatt bluntly said of him, "He must come down on one side of the fence or on the other."[25] Because of this he felt that the modern speech translations had in large measure taken the place of the commentaries, having the added advantage of not being liable to the commentator's atomistic peril.[26] Once the translator is freighted with such responsibility, it naturally follows that his work must be kept contemporary. Above all else, the making of modern speech translations must go on, for

> only in this way can the English New Testament be kept abreast of modern
> advances in grammar, lexicography, history, theology, and archaeology as
> they apply to the New Testament. They are the channel through which new
> light on the New Testament can most naturally and effectively be communi-
> cated to its readers. For the New Testament is no Christian *Book of the*

---

[22] *The Making of the English New Testament*, 114–15.

[23] Ibid., 117.

[24] Ibid., 116.

[25] James Moffatt, *The New Testament, A New Translation* (New York: Hodder and Stoughton, 1913) vii.

[26] E. J. Goodspeed, "The Versions of the New Testament," *Int* 3 (1949) 76.

Dead; it is a living and transforming force, an abiding voice, in short, the Word of God.[27]

The Goodspeed New Testament sought the commonplace not only in language but also in appearance. It was published to resemble any other book. The format was open page, single column, with modern paragraphing. As Weymouth before him, Goodspeed made the words of each speaker in the action a new paragraph. Neither division nor numbering of chapter and verse was permitted to invade the body of the text. The amount of text contained was summarized (e.g., 11:22–12:8) at the bottom of each page. The volume contained no marginal notes or footnotes of any kind. With few exceptions, Goodspeed closely followed the Greek text of Westcott and Hort.

The New Testament, An American Translation, was published in October, 1923. Looking back autobiographically, Goodspeed described his "horrendous deed" as follows:

> This simple act, obscurely done, in my own field of specialization, on the basis of many years of close study, with no expectation of any publicity at all, and quietly published at the University of Chicago Press, called forth from the public press a nationwide, indeed worldwide and vehement protest. . . .[28]

This immediate public reaction was owing to the circumstance that, led by Chicago newspapers, the national wire services prematurely issued samples of the translation from galley proofs during the late summer of 1923. Editorial writers and the letter writing public seized their pens to register their disapproval of what they read. Typical was this editorial in the *New York Times*, cuttingly entitled "The Bible a la Chicago":

> It is possible that the new translation of the Bible made by Professor Goodspeed of Chicago will be useful to students, but if the published excerpts are typical of the entire translation, there is little danger that it will replace the King James version. It may be more accurate, it undoubtedly uses more commonplace phrases. But readers of the Bible are less interested in precision of translation and in modernity of expression than they are in the terse richness which has made the King James version one of the great masterpieces of English. There is more in a phrase than many literalists can see. Long use gives it a connotation which may not be strictly in accordance with the original text, but which lends it force and meaning. . . . It is conceivable that some of these new phrases are more accurate—though even that is doubtful—and it is clear that some are more modern. But the difference in meaning or intelligibility between "inherit the earth" and "possess the land"; or between "the children of God" and "God's sons," is certainly so small that it fails to justify the substitution of ugly new phrases for the rich old words

---

[27] Ibid., 77.
[28] E. J. Goodspeed, *As I Remember*, 155.

which through long use have acquired a particular flavor. When it comes to the substitution of such words as "lamp" for "candle" and "peck measure" for "bushel" and "stand" for "candlestick," one is struck by the absurdity of endeavoring to "modernize" language. Had the translator been willing to "go whole hog," he would have written "electric light" instead of lamp, and "fixture" instead of stand.

The new version has a further demerit. Not content with would-be up-to-date phrases, it also goes in for modern verbosity. A single example illustrates this point. For the clear and forceful sentence in the King James version, "Think not that I am come to destroy the law, or the prophets: I am not come to destroy, but to fulfill," the Chicago Professor has written, "Do you suppose that I have come to do away with the Law or the Prophets. I have not come to do away with them but to enforce them."

For serious and scholarly studies of Hebrew and Greek texts with a view to eliminating inaccuracies of translation there will always be approval. But with attempts to "modernize" the language of the Bible by substituting for the vigorous and colorful language of the King James version such verbose and flat phraseology as is given in the published extracts from the new Chicago version there will be little sympathy.[29]

Goodspeed's recollection of this storm of criticism and protest constitutes one of the liveliest chapters in his autobiography.[30]

Peering through this storm, Goodspeed discerned the shape of two formidable opponents. One was the appalling ignorance of the history of the English Bible and of progress in biblical science displayed by the public press. The other was the massive resistance to change made by the zealous adherents of the King James Version. Much bewildered and a little angry, Goodspeed rose to do battle with both. Taking advantage of the notoriety created by his "bad" press, he launched a counterattack from lecture platforms from coast to coast. The form and content of his lectures soon became clear and fixed: a brief presentation of the case for translating the New Testament, spiced with a generous sampling of choice editorials and letters, and reinforced by a platform display of actual copies of the seven famous predecessors of the King James Version. More than one hundred such lectures were given during the first year of the translation's appearance.

Goodspeed has been criticized for writing as though most of his readers had only the Authorized Version.[31] The criticism is understandable but unfair. He was perfectly aware of the English and American revisions, much more so than his popular opposition. Moreover, while he appreciated their textual accuracy, he criticized their style and form. He disapproved of their translation method which he described as

---

[29] August 27, 1923, p. 10.
[30] *As I Remember*, 155–90.
[31] E. H. Robertson, *The New Translations of the Bible* (London: SCM Press, 1959) 88.

> the strange idea that in dealing with the Bible, one could translate a Greek
> word into English, and then another Greek word into English, and then
> another, and the completed product would mean what the Greek sentence
> had been intended to convey, without having had to pass through the mind
> of the translator.[32]

He also opposed their perpetuation of the chapter and verse divisions on the
principle that these 7,959 little paragraphs encouraged readers and interpre-
ters to piece them together at will, irrespective of their connection. Most of
all he deplored as an obstacle to understanding, the sixteenth century English that saturates all the traditional forms of the English Bible. In view of
his experience, however, one could scarcely blame Goodspeed if he had in
fact completely ignored all versions but the King James, for it was by that
version alone that the public weighed the American translation and found it
wanting. It was because the press and the public wrote as if no New Testament but the English Authorized Version had ever existed that Goodspeed
engaged in a lifelong effort to expose the facts.

His personal campaign began as soon as the reception of his work became clear. Hurt by the editorial writers whom he felt acted as though King
James himself were at their elbow, Goodspeed adopted his father's suggestion to take the case to the pages of the *Atlantic Monthly*. Thus, an article
entitled "The Ghost of King James" appeared in the January, 1924, issue of
the magazine.[33] The article began with an appeal for applying the great
American faith in progress to the modern advances in New Testament research. For is not the retranslation of the New Testament the most obvious
use of this new light and understanding? This is precisely what was done in
the American translation. Yet,

> in a hundred editorial sanctuaries, on the evening after the announcement,
> appeared the glowering ghost of King James, who never fails to rise and walk
> the earth when any new rendering of the New Testament has the temerity to
> show itself. He was not well-pleased with the new enterprise. 'Let it be
> anathema maranatha,' cried King James, who was never able to understand
> that 'maranatha' was not a curse but a blessing; and all the editors cried
> 'Amen!' and seized their fountain pens. Never was the literature of humor
> more rapidly enriched than in the moments that followed; and next morning
> from Utah to Manhattan there rose an editorial chorus of praise for good
> King James.[34]

This "chorus of praise" is then condemned on the following grounds: (1) the
editors conjured up the completely erroneous conception that a modern
translator simply cuts and alters the King James Version instead of working

---

[32] *New Chapters in New Testament Study*, 119.

[33] *Atlantic Monthly* 133 (1924) 71–76.

[34] Ibid., 72.

with the tools of modern biblical research; (2) the editors and their public assumed that the King James Bible they knew was unchanged from 1611, while the truth is that few verses remain unchanged (not to mention the quiet dropping of the entire Apocrypha); (3) modern discovery and the march of sound learning mean nothing to these men, for conventionality and tradition reign supreme; (4) the editors assume that King James is perfectly clear and intelligible, when in fact he has to be followed about by a commentator and an archaeologist to undo the impressions he has made, to say that when he says ghost he means spirit, and when he says candle he means lamp; (5) the editors are simply echoing the criticisms, condemnations, and curses that have been showered upon every translator of the New Testament from Jerome down; and (6) the two great claims made for the King James Version—that it is richly freighted with religious associations and that it is a noteworthy monument to sixteenth- and seventeenth-century English—may be admitted, but they do not outweigh the importance of understanding the meaning of the New Testament. The all-important freedom to understand the New Testament, concluded Goodspeed, "will never be gained for the English reader until we transfer our allegiance from the form and letter of the New Testament to its meaning and spirit, and thus lay forever the Ghost of King James."

So formidable a ghost was not to be laid with a single article, however, and Goodspeed struck again and again. His criticisms are woven through a chapter on the King James Version written the following year.[35] Ten years later he edited *The Translators to the Reader: Preface to the King James Version, 1611*,[36] containing the preface with modernized spelling, a facsimile of the preface in the first printing, and an essay[37] pleading the case for reprinting the preface with the King James Version today. Goodspeed felt that this was the only way to correct the prevalent fantastic misconceptions about the version, since the holders of these misconceptions will accept guidance about it from no one else but the men who made it. During the ensuing years he periodically repeated his criticisms until as recently as 1950.[38] Undoubtedly, the classic example of this remarkable crusade is an article dealing with the King James rendering "strain at a gnat" for "strain out a gnat" in Matthew 23:24.[39] Here the reader is confronted with a misprint to which people have become so attached that they actually prefer it to the original. Imagine the picture, he cried. On the one side, all the Greek manuscripts, ancient and medieval; all the ancient versions; all the printed editions of the Greek text; all the modern European versions; all the English

[35] E. J. Goodspeed, *The Making of the English New Testament*, 41–51.

[36] (Chicago: University of Chicago Press, 1935).

[37] Revised from an article of the same title in *Religion in Life* 1 (1932) 407–18.

[38] Cf. E. J. Goodspeed, *New Chapters in New Testament Study*, 102–26; *Problems of New Testament Translation*, 1–8; "The Present State of Bible Translation," *JBR* 18 (1950) 99–100.

[39] E. J. Goodspeed, "The Misprint that Made Good," *Religion in Life* 12 (1943) 205–10.

translations down to King James; all the English translations since King James; all the commentaries—these on the one side. And on the other, "this misprint, meaningless and unsupported." It is as if Goodspeed saw in this tiny error that defied correction a symbol of the large ghost that would not be laid!

To turn from the public reaction to the scholarly reception of the American translation is to encounter a very different attitude, for the learned biblical community fulfilled Goodspeed's expectations of a calm and quiet response. These were the men who were abreast of the advances of the biblical sciences and were aware of the facts concerning the King James Version. Being thoroughly acquainted with the revisions of 1881 and 1901 as well as the modern speech translations, they tended to regard the American translation as one more entry in the field. "Every translation has its own felicities," generalized one of the few early reviewers, "and this one is no exception."[40] In line with this attitude the learned journals gave the translation notice rather than critical review. As the translation was periodically reissued in different forms, these notices were repeated, being generally appreciative though not without reservation.[41] Historians of the English Bible, writing from the perspective of the years, were also appreciative. If few would declare with Goodspeed's colleagues that his version of the New Testament has no peer among modern speech translations,[42] most would agree that it is well worth study[43] and succeeds in capturing something of the freshness and modernity aimed at by the author.[44]

Perhaps the final word on the reception of Goodspeed's New Testament translation belongs to a unique combination of public and scholarly opinion. An unknown correspondent wrote a reviewer (F. F. Bruce) about his experience with the translation. He had received a copy of the Smith-Goodspeed Bible from an American serviceman in Calcutta during the war:

> I have found the translation free from harsh Americanisms, and apart from spelling variations find the poise, turn of speech and rhythmic flow of the language more 'English' than some of our more prominent home translations. Some of Dr. Goodspeed's renderings are singularly fortunate and I have found quite a stream of new light upon passages which are, in the Authorized Version dulled over by the archaic turn of speech. . . . Compared with

---

[40] "The New Testament—An American Translation," *ExpTim* 35 (1923) 110–11.

[41] Cf. F. C. Grant, *JR* 12 (1932) 373–74; H. B., *JBL* 63 (1944) 71; *Internationale kirchliche Zeitschrift* 39 (1949) 231–32, 240.

[42] Ira M. Price, *The Ancestry of Our English Bible* (3d rev. ed. W. A. Irwin and A. P. Wikgren; New York: Harper & Brothers, 1956) 298.

[43] G. Milligan, *The New Testament and Its Transmission* (London: Hodder and Stoughton, 1932) 178.

[44] Pope, *English Versions of the Bible*, 594.

Moffatt by and large I find Goodspeed far more real, more readable and, more important still, more satisfying.[45]

Commenting on the letter, Bruce adds: "I regard such an assessment, from an articulate but non-specialist representative of the class of reader (albeit an Englishman) for which the translation was designed, as more valuable in its way than any critical review by a scholar."[46]

Twenty-two years after his American translation appeared, Goodspeed published *Problems of New Testament Translation*,[47] a book which one reviewer characterized as "115 examples of the superiority of Goodspeed's translation of the New Testament to the King James."[48] Other reviewers described it as an *apologia* for his own and other modern speech translations.[49] All agreed that despite the more than two decades that separated this volume from the American translation, the two were, in reality, companion volumes. "Translation," Goodspeed concluded in the book's opening essay, "is a matter of infinite detail, sometimes so slight as to appear trivial. But in translation, no detail is trivial, for translation is made up of a wealth of such details, neglect of any one of which may vitiate the result."[50] The balance of the work illustrates the point. More than one hundred passages from the Greek New Testament are presented with a threefold enquiry made about each: (1) Where did the traditional readings of the King James and the revised versions originate? (2) How have modern translators dealt with them in private translations of the last century? (3) What is the present position of learning about them and what new light has been cast upon them by the Greek papyri, the Greek inscriptions and recent studies in Greek literature, lexicography and grammar?[51] Each discussion is concluded by the author's own suggested rendering. This book, in combination with the translation itself, affords the interested reader insight into some of the problems of New Testament translation as understood and practiced by one translator.

---

[45] Quoted by the recipient, F. F. Bruce, *History of the Bible in English* (New York: Oxford University Press, 1978) 172–73.

[46] Ibid., 173.

[47] (Chicago: University of Chicago Press, 1945).

[48] Morton S. Enslin, *Crozer Quarterly* 22 (1945) 284.

[49] Edwin D. Sanders, *TS* 6 (1945) 441; Allen P. Wikgren, *JR* 26 (1946) 62.

[50] *Problems of New Testament Translation*, 8.

[51] Ibid., vii.

IV

THE APOCRYPHA:
TRANSLATION AND RELATED STUDIES

The Apocrypha is, to use the words of J. Isaacs, "the Cinderella of Bible translation."[1] Luther insulted it, Coverdale apologized for it, the Puritans persecuted it and the Bible reading public ignored it. The attitudes and events underlying such phrases have been related in many books and require only a brief summary here. The designation of certain biblical books as Apocryphal is commonly traced to the judgment of the Latin scholar Jerome. In Palestine he discovered that the Greek Old Testament contained more books than were recognized by the Hebrew canon. The problem thus encountered was resolved by a dual decision: as a churchman, Jerome left the excess books in his Latin Bible; as a scholar he designated them as Apocryphal. In his usage the term marked "the fundamental distinction between the canonical Scriptures and the books which, though of an edifying nature, were not to be used to establish doctrine."[2] Some eleven centuries passed before Martin Luther capped this judgment of Jerome by gathering together the Apocryphal books and placing them in a special section at the end of the Old Testament.

The first printed English Bible was issued by Miles Coverdale in 1535, and with its appearance the Apocrypha entered the history of the English versions. Coverdale followed the example of Luther in the disposition of the Apocryphal books, as did all subsequent Protestant English Bibles up to and including the version of 1611. In all of these the Apocryphal books form a separate group, placed "in a sort of ghetto between the Old Testament and the New."[3] The earlier English versions repeated Jerome's distinction between canonical and Apocryphal writings, but by 1611 this practice had ceased and the books in question were simply headed Apocrypha. The fact that the very inclusion of these books between the covers of the Bible was becoming a matter of controversy, however, is indicated by an ordinance of the Archbishop of Canterbury in 1615, making the publishing of Bibles

[1] *Ancient and English Versions of the Bible*, ed. H. W. Robinson (Oxford: Clarendon Press, 1940) 217.

[2] B. M. Metzger, *An Introduction to the Apocrypha* (New York: Oxford University Press, 1957) 179–80.

[3] C. C. Torrey, *The Apocryphal Literature* (New Haven: Yale University Press, 1945) 4.

without the Apocrypha punishable by a year's imprisonment. The Puritans continued to object to these books on the basis of their moral and religious content and demanded copies of their own Geneva Version without them. Although the Church of England was equally insistent that the Apocryphal books were part of the Bible, the rising Puritan and evangelical influence served to push them farther into the background. These latter forces won the victory when, in 1827, the British and Foreign Bible Society decided to stop circulating Bibles which included the Apocrypha. This decision was promptly adopted by the American Bible Society and was shortly thereafter reflected in the policies of commercial publishers. Soon English Bibles with the Apocrypha became so rare that the contents of the latter came to be unknown to the general public.

This lack of interest in the Apocrypha was more demonstrated than it was altered by the English Revisers of 1881–85. An extension of their work to include a revision of the Apocrypha does not appear to have been contemplated by the authorizing Convocation.[4] That it was ultimately included in the revision plan was a result of copyright negotiations. In the course of 1872 the Committee of Convocation and the representatives of the University Presses of Oxford and Cambridge entered into an agreement whereby the latter, on condition of acquiring the copyright of the Revised Version, agreed to provide a sum sufficient to cover the cost of production. It was then for the first time stipulated that the Apocrypha should be included in the total task of revision. The fact that the revision of the Apocrypha was, as Lupton points out, an afterthought serves to underline the extent of the degradation endured by those books.

When, in the third decade of the twentieth century, Goodspeed surveyed the scene, the situation had only changed in one respect: from the time of the appearance of the Revised Version, voices had been raised on behalf of a better translation of the Apocrypha. The *Expository Times* described the Revised Version of 1894 as the best edition and the most lucid explanation of the Apocrypha ever published. Yet its makers had seriously erred in outdoing even the Old and New Testament revisers in the retention of obsolete forms from the Authorized Version. It is a fine product of modern reverence and modern scholarship, concludes the critic, but "may some later time come when materials will be found and men will be found to do it better."[5] Lupton concludes his essay on the English Revision with these words: "On the whole, a study of the RV of the Apocr. cannot fail to make us aware of the great amount of work still to be done before such a translation as we desire to see can be produced: work in settling the text, in harmonizing proper names, in

---

[4] J. H. Lupton, *A Dictionary of the Bible*, ed. J. Hastings, 5 (New York: Charles Scribner's Sons, 1904) 262ff.

[5] *ExpTim* 7 (1895/96) 331f.

elucidating obscure passages."[6] Even more to the point are these words of
F. C. Grant, written in a review of *The Bible, An American Translation*:

> It is not very gracious to accept a gift and ask for more, but one cannot help
> hoping that the Chicago translators will proceed next to give us the Apoc-
> rypha in "an American translation." Those books certainly need to be pre-
> sented in modern guise. They are more and more widely read every year
> and a fresh readable translation based upon accurate scholarship would be a
> great boon to students everywhere.[7]

The extent to which Goodspeed was influenced by such voices is difficult to evaluate. It is possible, however, to cull from his own writings a number of the points which did motivate him to produce a new translation.

In the Preface to *The Apocrypha, An American Translation*[8] and in
the opening chapter of *The Story of the Apocrypha*,[9] Goodspeed traced the
major events which led to the exclusion of these books from the English
Bible. His personal opinion of this neglect found expression in these lines
from still another source:

> It has been truly said that no one can have the complete Bible, as a source
> book for the cultural study of art, literature, history and religion, without the
> Apocrypha. From the earliest Christian times down to the age of the King
> James Version, they belonged to the Bible; and, while modern critical judg-
> ments and religious attitudes deny them a position of equality with the Old
> and New Testament scriptures, historically and culturally they are still an
> integral part of the Bible.[10]

Goodspeed's conviction that the Apocryphal books were necessary to render
any Bible complete offers more than adequate motivation for translating
them for inclusion in his own American version.

Moreover, he pointed out that the translation of the Apocrypha always
lagged behind that of the Old Testament, and especially of the New. In his
version of 1535, for example, Coverdale made no pretense of translating the
Apocrypha from the Greek. He simply translated them from the Latin with
the aid of recent German versions. The Thomas Matthew Bible of 1537
reproduced Coverdale in the Apocrypha, and those books continued to rest
on Latin and German versions in the Great Bible of 1539. The Geneva Bible
of 1560 offered a revised Apocrypha and in some cases made new translations of books from Greek. The Bishops' Bible of 1568 and the King James

---

[6] *A Dictionary of the Bible*, 269.

[7] *ATR* 18 (1936) 51.

[8] (Chicago: University of Chicago Press, 1938) v–vi.

[9] (Chicago: University of Chicago Press, 1939) 1–12.

[10] *The Complete Bible, An American Translation*, by J. M. P. Smith and E. J. Goodspeed
(Chicago: University of Chicago Press, 1939) v.

Bible followed the earlier versions of the Apocrypha, revising them cautiously in the light of the Greek. Further new translations from Greek into English were produced by the makers of the Revised Version of 1894, but a considerable portion of that version continued to rest upon the Latin version Coverdale first translated for his Bible in 1535. In the course of the nineteenth century, the Septuagint was translated into English by Charles Thomson (1808) and Sir Lancelot Brenton (1844), but neither included the Apocryphal books. The group of scholars working under the editorial supervision of R. H. Charles[11] also failed to produce a fresh translation of the entire Apocrypha. While more than half translated the books assigned them, a minority were content to reprint the Revised Version. "So," concludes Goodspeed, "while individual books have here and there been translated by highly competent scholars, there has been no translation of the Greek Apocrypha directly into English throughout, until the American translation of 1938."[12] The manner in which Goodspeed emphasized this point at every opportunity indicates that the pioneering nature of his undertaking provided no small measure of motivation.

The criticism heaped upon his New Testament translation had provided Goodspeed with firsthand knowledge of the restrictions the traditional English Bible placed upon a biblical translator's freedom. There was, Goodspeed noted, not even this reason for leaving the Apocrypha in the archaic dress of sixteenth-century English. The familiar arguments for the standard translations, that their language is so poetic and so familiar and so freighted with religious associations, had no bearing here. Few people knew what the Apocryphal books were, much less what they contained. Therefore, the Apocrypha offered a fair field for retranslation in which the scholar could freely use his skills.

Mention has been made of Goodspeed's contention that a Bible without the Apocrypha is incomplete. It should be noted here that he recognized in the Apocrypha a number of values besides completeness: The Prayer of Manasseh he regarded as a notable piece of liturgy; 1 Maccabees has great historical value for its story of Judaism in the second century before Christ; the additions to Esther impart a religious color to that romantic story; and Wisdom and Ecclesiasticus are among the masterpieces of the Jewish sages. But above all else, Goodspeed judged this appendix to the Old Testament to be so important and necessary a link between the Old Testament and the New, that if there were no Old Testament at all, the Apocrypha would still be indispensable to the student of the New Testament, of which they form the prelude and the background:

---

[11] *The Apocrypha and Pseudepigrapha of the Old Testament,* ed. R. H. Charles, 1. (Oxford: Clarendon Press, 1913).

[12] *The Story of the Apocrypha* (Chicago: University of Chicago Press, 1939) 11.

This is why I have prepared an American translation of the Apocrypha, to complete an American translation of the Bible, and to make its various books more intelligible to college and university students and to the general reader. The strong contrast they present in sheer moral values to the New Testament is most instructive. And they form an indispensable part of the historic Christian Bible, as it was known in the ancient Greek and Latin churches, in the Reformation and the Renaissance, and in all Authorized English Bibles, Catholic and Protestant.[13]

Although it was not above criticism, Goodspeed's American translation was a valuable contribution to the literature on the Apocrypha. From the time of its publication until the appearance of the Revised Standard Version, it satisfied the long felt need for a readable and convenient English version of these books. The fact that when the makers of the Revised Standard Version published the results of their labors in 1957 they were obliged to acknowledge their indebtedness not only to the King James and English Revised Versions but also to Goodspeed's translation of 1938 indicates some measure of its stature. Moreover, the American translation continues to have a life quite independent of its contribution to the Revised Standard Version, for as recently as 1959 it was reissued in a popular paperback edition (including an Introduction to the Apocrypha by Moses Hadas)[14] which seems destined for a continuing circulation among the students and general readers for whom it was prepared.

The contribution of Edgar Goodspeed in the area of Apocryphal literature was not limited to translation. He included brief chapters on the Old Testament Apocrypha in *The Story of the Old Testament*[15] and in *How Came the Bible?*[16] Of these two essays the former is the more significant, not only because it offers a preview of many positions destined to be expanded by the author at a later date but also because it indicates that Goodspeed was then convinced that the Apocryphal books were part of the Old Testament story. As such the chapter pointed toward the subsequent translation and a more serious introduction. The latter appeared in 1939 under the title, *The Story of the Apocrypha*.[17] "This book," writes Goodspeed, "is intended to bring the main facts as to the origin of the collection and of the several books concisely before the student and the general reader, to enable

---

[13] *The Apocrypha, An American Translation* (Chicago: University of Chicago Press, 1938) vi–vii.

[14] E. J. Goodspeed, *The Apocrypha, An American Translation* (New York: Random House, 1959): "More recently (1957) a Revised Standard Version Apocrypha has been prepared by a committee of American scholars. But the freshness and directness of Professor Goodspeed's version and its closer approach to a dignified vernacular make it more desirable for the general reader, and it has therefore been chosen for presentation in the present volume" (xxvi).

[15] (Chicago: University of Chicago Press, 1934) 167–78.

[16] (New York: Abingdon-Cokesbury Press, 1940) 48–58.

[17] (Chicago: University of Chicago Press.)

him more readily to gain from them what they have to contribute for literature, history, and religion."[18] Chapters devoted to the individual books of the
Apocrypha are supplemented with sections dealing with the Apocrypha in
the Bible, the New Testament, and the Christian Church.

The Story of the Apocrypha was warmly received. "There can be no
question of the excellence of the work as a whole," wrote E. F. Scott, "or of
the service it renders to the student of the Bible. . . . There could be no
more attractive introduction to them [The Apocrypha] than this volume of
Professor Goodspeed's."[19] W. F. Stinespring described "this popular and very
readable account of the Apocryphal books" as "a distinct service to the pop-
ularization of Biblical science."[20]

The Story of the Apocrypha does indeed represent a substantial contribution in the area of Apocryphal studies, particularly in the United States.
The only comparable handbooks available to the general reader at the time
were the English publications of W. O. E. Oesterley[21] (although it was somewhat too technical for the purpose) and R. H. Malden.[22] The appearance of
Goodspeed's volume as a companion to his American translation published
the previous year had the same reciprocating impact in the thirties as the
Revised Standard Version of the Apocrypha and the related An Introduction to the Apocrypha by B. M. Metzger have had since their synchronized
appearance. Indeed, it is not unlikely that Goodspeed's publications on the
Apocrypha played a significant role in creating and sustaining the interest
which has resulted in the Revised Standard Version and the handy introductions which have now largely superceded his own.[23]

During the years of his study of early Christian literature, Goodspeed
became acquainted with a considerable number of writings claiming to be
genuine documents of Christian antiquity. Some of these books and tracts
came to his attention from obscure private sources, while others were
brought to him by students and colleagues who desired information about
them. In the thought that a useful service might be rendered by describing
them together and pointing out their failure to meet the simple and familiar
tests of antiquity and genuineness, Goodspeed published information on

---

[18] Ibid., viii.

[19] JR 20 (1940) 100.

[20] JBL 59 (1940) 537f.

[21] An Introduction to the Books of the Apocrypha (London: S.P.C.K., 1935).

[22] The Apocrypha (London: Oxford University Press, 1936).

[23] In addition to the cited works of W. O. E. Oesterley (reprinted in 1953) and B. M.
Metzger, cf. R. C. Dentan, The Apocrypha, Bridge of the Testaments (Greenwich,
Connecticut: Seabury Press, 1954), L. H. Brockington, A Critical Introduction to the
Apocrypha (London: Gerald Duckworth & Co., 1961), R. F. Surburg, Introduction to the Inter-
testamental Period (St. Louis: Concordia Publishing House, 1975) and N. De Lange,
Apocrypha: Jewish Literature of the Hellenistic Age (New York: The Viking Press, 1978).

several of them under the title, *Strange New Gospels*.[24] The appearance of this book led to the discovery of as many more specimens of such literature, some of which Goodspeed described in *New Chapters in New Testament Study*.[25] In 1956 he returned to this subject once more, assembling and bringing up to date his earlier discussions of these bizarre texts and adding some new ones of very recent origin, in a volume entitled *Modern Apocrypha*.[26]

The identification of this literary corpus was not rendered easier by Goodspeed's application to it of a term which has become extremely confusing. Apocrypha, as commonly defined, "refers to a nucleus of fourteen or fifteen documents, written during the last two centuries before Christ and the first century of the Christian era."[27] Obviously these are not the Apocrypha under discussion. Besides the Old Testament Apocrypha proper there was a vast body of literature in circulation in Judaism, written between 300 B.C. and A.D. 120 under the names of ancient worthies of Israel, to which is generally attached the term "Pseudepigrapha."[28] Although this latter term is applied by some scholars to the false and spurious books which early circulated under prominent Christian names, M. R. James chose to call them *The Apocryphal New Testament*.[29] The relationship between the latter volume and Goodspeed's *Modern Apocrypha* is still more confusing. In general, the same documents are not discussed; but several which are described by Goodspeed are mentioned by James, and in one instance the latter does print a version of a text.[30] For the most part, however, the literature discussed by Goodspeed is both too late and too fantastic to be included in *The Apocryphal New Testament*. On the whole, *Strange New Gospels* was a less confusing title.

The attitude of the scholarly world toward these documents is ably expressed by M. R. James and M. S. Enslin. The former writes:

---

[24] (Chicago: University of Chicago Press, 1931). The documents dealt with are: The Unknown Life of Jesus Christ; The Aquarian Gospel; The Crucifixion of Jesus, by an Eyewitness; Pilate's Court, and the Archko Volume; The Confession of Pontius Pilate; The Letter of Benan; The Twenty-ninth Chapter of Acts; The Letter of Jesus Christ.

[25] (New York: Macmillan, 1937) 189–219. Documents here treated are: The Letter from Heaven; The Gospel of Josephus; The Book of Jasher; The Lost Books of the Bible.

[26] (Boston: Beacon Press). In addition to most of the documents dealt with in the two earlier works, the following also are discussed: The Description of Christ; The Death Warrant of Jesus Christ; The Long-Lost Second Book of Acts; Oahspe; The Nazarene Gospel. *Modern Apocrypha* was reprinted under the title *Famous "Biblical" Hoaxes* (Grand Rapids: Baker Book House, 1956).

[27] Metzger, *Introduction to the Apocrypha*, 3.

[28] Charles, *Apocrypha and Pseudepigrapha*, viii.

[29] (Oxford: Clarendon Press, 1924) xiii–xiv. Cf. Edgar Hennecke's title, *New Testament Apocrypha*, ed. W. Schneemelcher (Philadelphia: The Westminster Press, 1963, 1965), whose two volumes have superceded the work of James.

[30] Ibid., the Letter of Lentulus, 477–78. This is Goodspeed's "The Description of Christ."

Three other modern forgeries about the Life Of Christ I will just name—more to show my consciousness of their existence than because they are at all interesting. One is a life said to have been found in a Buddhist monastery in Tibet, and connected with the name of Notovitch as discoverer or translator. The second is a ridiculous and disgusting American book called 'The Archko Volume'. The third is the Letter of Benan (an Egyptian physician), shown by Professor Carl Schmidt (*Der Benanbrief*, 1919) to have been forged by Ernst Edler von der Planitz. This, I believe, had a great vogue recently in Central Europe, but I have never heard of it in an English dress.[31]

Again:

One famous apocryphal Epistle will not be produced here, viz. The Letter of Christ concerning Sunday, extant in almost every European language and in many Oriental versions. It was fabled to have fallen on the altar at Jerusalem, Rome, Constantinople—where not?—and is a long, very dull denunciation of what we call Sabbath-breaking, with threats of disaster to the transgressors.[32]

In an article on New Testament Apocrypha, Enslin mentions the numerous modern apocrypha, still appearing to perplex and excite the hopes of many uninformed readers that priceless discoveries have but recently been made available: "Without exception they are worthless trash and the rankest forgeries."[33]

Goodspeed was fully aware of the fact that these modern apocrypha have been for the most part judged unworthy of serious consideration.[34] He would readily concur but for the extravagant claims made for them. When people are being misled by them, he argues, it is time to put fastidiousness aside and state the facts. Comparing these frauds with the genuine discovery of the Dead Sea Scrolls, he concludes:

In contrast to such discoveries, the pieces dealt with in this book, for all their claims of antiquity, cannot stand the tests of scholarly research. Indeed it is often the case with these curious frauds that when they first appear they are promptly unmasked; but a generation, or a century, later, long after their exposure has been forgotten, they are revived by somebody and make a fresh bid for acceptance. I think it lamentable that people who ask for light on such pieces cannot be at once referred to a book that will clear it all up without prejudice and quite objectively. This field has been simply ignored by American scholarship. Hence this book.[35]

---

[31] Ibid., 90.
[32] Ibid., 476.
[33] *IDB*, 1. 168.
[34] *Modern Apocrypha* (Boston: Beacon Press, 1956) vi ff.
[35] Ibid., viii–ix.

Proceeding on the assumption that the most satisfactory method of enlightening a public which takes these documents seriously is to subject them to serious criticism, Goodspeed carefully sifts and weighs the external and internal evidence of their authenticity. The representative discussion of The Aquarian Gospel, in summary form, illustrates the result.[36] After explaining the fantastic astrological notion which underlies its title, Goodspeed moves on to the matters of authorship and origin. The author is identified as Levi H. Dowling (1844–1911). Dowling believed he was able to explore the past unerringly by coming into harmony with the rhythms and vibrations of certain mysterious imperishable records of life preserved in the Supreme Intelligence. The Aquarian Gospel is the record of his communications thus obtained in California during the early hours of the morning. Although the subjective character of materials obtained in this way is immediately apparent to the critical mind, Goodspeed observes that this document, published in Los Angeles in 1911, had by 1954 reached its twenty-first printing.

Any estimation of the net worth of these studies hinges upon the answer to the question: Are they worth doing? Goodspeed's ready concurrence in the judgment that this literature possesses no intrinsic value obviously moves the decision to the validity of his contention that its perennial popularity necessitates a permanent critical refutation. Inasmuch as the most vehement detractors of modern apocrypha admit to their incredible circulation, Goodspeed's argument must stand. *Modern Apocrypha* remains a contribution to the religious education of the general public if for no other reason than that it had for so long no competitors. M. R. James notices a few of these writings but dismisses them with a line or two. A few of the individual pieces have been investigated in Europe. In his article, Enslin lists a few of their titles "as an indication that the wildfires of imagination are still burning, though with but a smoky flame," and ends by declaring: "None of these trivia is discussed in separate articles in this dictionary."[37] It is significant that the lone bibliographical references which he makes for modern apocryphal writings are to Goodspeed's *Modern Apocrypha* and *Strange New Gospels*. To the present these studies remain a unique contribution by a competent authority.

---

[36] Ibid., 15–19. Cf. *Strange New Gospels* (Chicago: University of Chicago Press, 1931) 25–30.
[37] *IDB*, 1. 168.

V

THE SEMITIC-HELLENISTIC DEBATE

The thirties and forties of the twentieth century were marked by a learned controversy concerning the original language of much of the New Testament. The Semitic or Aramaic hypothesis which came to be linked especially with the name of Charles Cutler Torrey stemmed from a reexamination of the Greek of the New Testament. New Testament students contemporary with Torrey were undertaking such examinations from the side of the increased knowledge of Hellenistic Greek gained from the papyrus discoveries. Their investigations were laying to rest the so-called "biblical Greek." Many peculiarities of vocabulary and syntax, once put down to the influence of the Septuagint and the Hebrew or Aramaic dialects of Palestine, were now held to belong to the inner development of the koine Greek itself. Torrey, on the other hand, approached the character of New Testament Greek from the Semitic side and soon joined the company of Semitic scholars who held the theory of written Semitic sources underlying a considerable portion of the synoptic Gospels. In his hands the theory was eventually extended to include the Fourth Gospel, Acts 1–15, and the Apocalypse. The balance of the New Testament Torrey left to the Greek specialists.

The language of the four Gospels as they have come down to us was, in Torrey's opinion, a Greek of peculiar character. The evidence from the papyri may indicate that the farmer of the Fayum spoke a Greek essentially identical with that of the synoptic evangelists, but

> that it even remotely resembled the language *in which they wrote their Gospels* is not true at all. No evidence which has thus far come to light tends to show that such Greek as that of the Gospels was ever spoken in any part of the world. The idiom of the synoptic Gospels, like that of the Apocalypse, is half Semitic throughout.[1]

Despite the fact that the Gospels are attributed to different men writing at different times and places and for different audiences, they all present this curious jargon, half Semitic, half Greek. One early explanation of this mongrel Greek laid the phenomenon to the speech of half-educated Galilean

---

[1] C. C. Torrey, "The Translations Made from the Original Aramaic Gospels," *Studies in the History of Religions presented to Crawford Howell Toy*, ed. D. G. Lyon and G. F. Moore (New York: The Macmillan Company, 1912) 274.

fishermen. Another explained it by appeals to ignorance or bad taste or both. Others put it down to the circumstance that the evangelists had (supposedly) no idea they were writing literature, and still others to the influence of the Septuagint. The most popular explanation in Torrey's day was that the evangelists wrote in Greek but thought in Semitic. These theses, he contended, are all shattered by the consideration that the New Testament documents are the work of men of culture and literary resource whose mother tongue was Greek. Moreover, two of the evangelists offer extensive specimens of Greek quite different in character from the mixed idiom of their Gospels. The pure idiom of Luke 1:1–4 differs greatly from the mixture encountered from 1:5 on. Does this mean, asked Torrey, that the author thought in Greek some of the time and in Aramaic the rest? In the Fourth Gospel, chapter 21 differs from the rest of the book in that it is pure Greek. It is as if after twenty chapters of literary bondage the evangelist is finally free to compose in his own style. Thus is the way prepared for Torrey's own explanation: if the language of the Gospels was not freely composed, the natural hypothesis is that it was translated. The character of Semitic Greek is well understood from the Septuagint. The Septuagint is a literal translation, or half a translation. Its vocabulary is Greek but its syntax is Hebrew. The resulting idiom is never Greek but always a mixture. The fundamental reason for this strange translation Greek lay in the translators' conception of their task:

> The original was not conceived in Greek, but in Hebrew or Aramaic, and what they were required to do was to present the same document *in a Greek dress*; this was the only way they could make it accessible to Greek readers, and at the same time let it speak for itself. This was the typical attitude of the ancient translator, irrespective of the nature of the text he rendered.[2]

What is said here of the Septuagint is equally true for the language of the Gospels—with the difference that (aside from Luke 1 and 2, and the Old Testament quotations which are Hebrew) the syntax throughout is Aramaic. Therefore, said Torrey, "the general conclusion as to the documents of the New Testament whose Greek has a distinct and continuous Semitic tinge is this, that they were translated; no other conclusion is justified by the evidence which is at present available."[3]

William F. Albright judged that it would be difficult to imagine a more complete *volte-face* than would be necessary for New Testament criticism if Torrey's views were proved correct.

> He has consequently been attacked with the greatest vigor by many New Testament scholars, led by E. J. Goodspeed and D. W. Riddle. Other scholars, few of whom are specialists in the New Testament, have rallied to his

---

[2] Ibid., 279.
[3] Ibid., 287.

support, but the majority remains on the sidelines, equally awed by Torrey's learning and impressed by the authority of his antagonists.[4]

There is justification for Albright's description of Goodspeed as the leader of Torrey's critics, for his published opposition spanned more than twenty years and challenged the Aramaic hypothesis at every point.

That the New Testament was written in Greek seemed to Goodspeed an obvious fact. Yet he observed that this position was being subjected to wide attack: R. B. Y. Scott had published a doctoral dissertation maintaining that the Apocalypse of John was a translation from a Hebrew original; C. F. Burney had affirmed that the Fourth Gospel was written in Aramaic; C. C. Torrey had begun by making the first part of Acts the translation of an Aramaic document and ended by extending the Aramaic predicate to the four Gospels; and a Syrian Christian, George Lamsa, had affirmed that the canonical Gospels were originally written in Syriac which he preferred to call Aramaic. Goodspeed observed that such notions were at least as old as Jerome, who declared that 1 Peter was originally written in Aramaic, thus making the Greek letter a translation. What was making the modern Aramaic school more significant for the Greek New Testament than the ancients was its endorsement by a distinguished group of scholars which included J. A. Montgomery, M. Burrows, C. W. Knopf, W. L. Phelps and Anson Phelps Stokes. These university men were hailing the neo-Aramaic movement as "epoch-making," and its leading spirit as a modern Erasmus. "In the presence of such a campaign on the part of Professors of Semitics, Classics and English," wrote Goodspeed, "perhaps specialists in New Testament Greek may be permitted to take a hand, more especially as it is the Greek New Testament, after all, that is under discussion."[5] That announced participation involved a general disagreement with the Semitists in the areas of philology, history and methodology, as well as specific criticism of their positions regarding the books of the New Testament.

In taking a hand in the debate as a specialist in New Testament Greek, Goodspeed was aware that his opponents would declare him incompetent to judge things Semitic. He declared that the New Testament writers were ignorant of Semitics. He pointed out that his own graduate work in New Testament had been preceded by three solid years of specialization in pure Semitics—Hebrew, Arabic, Assyrian, Aramaic, Babylonian, Syriac and Ethiopic.[6] With all the authority that this background could provide Goodspeed maintained that the language of the Gospels was vernacular Greek, meaning thereby the Greek of the papyri as pointed out by Deissmann and discovered afresh by Grenfell and Hunt at Oxyrhynchus and Tebtunis:

---

[4] *From the Stone Age to Christianity* (Baltimore: Johns Hopkins Press, 1940) 294–95.
[5] *New Chapters in New Testament Study* (New York: Macmillan, 1937) 130f.
[6] "The Possible Aramaic Gospel," *JNES* 1 (1942) 337n.

Many unusual constructions in New Testament Greek used to be explained as Semitisms—that is, as due to imitation of Hebrew and Aramaic idioms. But in the presence of the Greek papyri these too have rapidly dwindled until they have lost any possible literary significance. It has become clear that New Testament Greek is not a kind of ancient Yiddish, as some have supposed. The thousands of Greek papyrus documents from the very years of its origin have definitely established its right to be, and against the protests of classicists and Semitists, have recovered for it its rightful position, of which it had long been disinherited. The Gospels were written not in muddy Greek or an awkward patois. They were, rather, masterpieces of popular literature, the first books written in popular Greek.[7]

The kinship of the Greek of the New Testament with the vernacular of the papyri, he claimed, becomes increasingly clear. Scholars now possess definitely dated papyrus documents from every single year of the first century—not late copies but originals. By contrast, not one single Aramaic text from anywhere in that century, or even a copy of one, has been found. For him the evidence pointed toward one general conclusion:

New Testament philology, so long a debatable land between classical and Semitic realms, which made occasional raids upon it, but no complete survey of it, has emerged, by reason of the papyri, as a relatively independent discipline, dealing with the rise of a great popular religious Greek literature in the spoken language, which it employed for literary purposes with all the vivacity of the old Greek genius directed to new and nobler ends.[8]

Goodspeed's historical objections were every bit as integral to his argument as were his linguistic disagreements. Not only did the linguistic evidence indicate that the New Testament books in question *were* not written in Aramaic, the literary-historical situation decreed that they *could* not have been so written. He laid down three factors necessary for the production of a New Testament book or any other book: (1) an author, (2) a situation and (3) a public. While (1) and (2) are commonly recognized, Goodspeed stressed (3) as a particularly valuable safeguard against

conjecturally postulating precarious hypothetical documents, for which no probable public can be discerned. To every conjectural document we can apply these tests: Is the author whom it implies a reasonably probable historical figure? Is the situation or occasion which it implies historically probable? And can we reasonably postulate for it a public considerable enough to have taken it up and given it at least a brief life?[9]

[7] "The Original Language of the Gospels," *Atlantic Monthly* 154 (1934) 478.
[8] *New Chapters in New Testament Study*, 167–68.
[9] "The Origin of Acts," *JBL* 39 (1920) 85.

In Goodspeed's judgment, the conjectured Aramaic originals failed on all three counts. First, there were no authors for such documents, because Aramaic produced no literature. Second, in this period of Palestinian history, the Jews did not write books. They had plenty to say, and they said it, but they had a strong repugnance to written composition. Third, there was no Aramaic reading public, for there was nothing for them to read. What made any other view appear tenable, he believed, was a failure to distinguish between:

(1) Translation and composition: That Aramaic was used to translate Hebrew Scriptures does not make it a *literary* language. The Bible, or portions, has been translated into some 900 languages but there are not 900 literatures! To speak of the Aramaic Targums as though they were creative literature is quite misleading. Translating a text from one language to another is one thing; composing an original work is another. That pens and words are used in both operations is only a superficial resemblance.

(2) Oral and written transmission: When the translation was not written, but memorized, even the superficial resemblance disappears. Oral transmission exists in the mind—not on paper. Its very existence represents an aversion to literary creativity.

(3) Hebrew (the dead, sacred, literary, classical language) and the vernacular Aramaic: Even the scribal interpretation of the Law had to be in Hebrew, not Aramaic. So far was Aramaic from being recognized by the Jews as a literary vehicle.[10]

As the critical reaction to the Aramaic hypothesis indicates, it was a rare scholar who found no fault with Torrey's methodology. Many discovered more than one weakness. Under Goodspeed's scrutiny the Aramaic school of Gospel origins exhibited twelve general defects of method which made the securing of sound results impossible:

1. It disregards all the results of New Testament study in the fields of text, canon, literature, history, introduction and criticism, dismissing them as worthless without examination.
2. It fails to establish any such literary activity as it assumes in Aramaic in the period in question.
3. It offers no contemporary literary material by which to establish the Hebrew or Aramaic usages it claims.
4. It supplies few specific references to Semitic sources to satisfy scholars that the various words and forms it posits exist.
5. It omits from consideration all the Greek papyrus material, declaring it without examination to be of no significance.
6. It makes sweeping and unsupported assertions as to the Greek of the New Testament and, when these are challenged and disproved with accompanying evidences, gives no heed.

[10] *New Chapters in New Testament Study*, 139–40.

7. It fails to distinguish between oral and written composition.
8. It does not clearly distinguish translational from creative literary activity.
9. It weaves together items of various Semitic tongues—Arabic, Hebrew, Syriac, etc., to produce the words and forms it then argues from as recognized and established Aramaic usage.
10. It resorts to elaborate and remote Semitic explanations of words which are in ordinary use in the Greek papyri.
11. It does not scruple to present rejected Greek readings where they serve its turn, at the same time claiming to use the critical text of Westcott and Hort.
12. While distinctly declaring its repudiation of modern colloquial idiom in principle, it employs it in the text in almost every line.[11]

Torrey's treatment of Mark 7:3 is selected to demonstrate the lack of objective validity in this method. The word at issue is the Greek πυγμῇ, "with the fist," which the Aramaic school described as an amusing mistranslation of the Aramaic לִגְמַר , "at all." But, argued Goodspeed, this passage is, by hypothesis, manifestly one of the parenthetical explanations of Jewish customs to Gentile readers inserted by the Greek translator for their enlightenment. As such, it was composed in Greek, not Aramaic. Yet it yields just as readily to retranslation into Aramaic as any part of the Gospels. A method that works just as well on original Greek as on "translation" Greek is useless. On the other hand, should the Aramaic school deny that this parenthesis was supplied by the translator, but was a part of the original Aramaic Gospel, they must abandon the position that makes the Gospels Palestinian originals for Jewish readers. Thus, charged Goodspeed, Mark 7:3 either "proves that their method is invalid, or that the Gospel of Mark was written outside Palestine. It does not matter much which horn of the dilemma they take; the effect is the same—the overthrow of their position."

In view of the abundant literature published in the course of the Semitic-Hellenistic debate, the importance of the contribution of one man may not be immediately apparent. The extensive critical reaction to that hypothesis immediately dispels any notion that Goodspeed was engaged in a lone struggle. Contributions to the discussion were as rich and varied as the participation in it. Nevertheless, the criticism offered by Goodspeed was so broad, sustained and emphatic in nature, that there is a certain propriety in the place of leadership ascribed to him by W. F. Albright.

From the vantage point of the perspective now obtained, it is possible to assess some of the strengths and weaknesses of Goodspeed's contribution to the Semitic-Hellenistic debate.

---

[11] Ibid., 156–57.

There can be no doubt, for example, that both his position and its influence were significantly enhanced by the circumstances of his early training in Semitics. It will be recalled that his graduate work in New Testament had been preceded by three years of specialization in pure Semitics—Hebrew, Arabaic, Assyrian, Aramaic, Babylonian, Syriac and Ethiopic. Having begun his technical training in the field of Old Testament, he was, among New Testament specialists, uniquely equipped to challenge Torrey on his own ground. Where other scholars were forced by linguistic limitations to accept Torrey's examples of Semitic coloring, Aramaic idiom and mistranslation, Goodspeed felt free to render critical judgments with confidence and authority. This in itself made him a spokesman for the New Testament side of the debate. It is, of course, impossible to measure the extent of his influence on his New Testament colleagues, but it seems safe to assume that it was considerable.

Further, Goodspeed's position that the Gospels, Acts 1–15 and the Apocalypse *would* not have been written in Palestine was carefully argued. At one place he wrote concerning Christianity: "It was the *Greek* world that first welcomed and understood it, and that adopted it and set it on its way. Its use of the Greek language was only a symbol of a far deeper affinity."[12] One detects here an almost theological sympathy for the correctness of the Hellenistic position. It is simply the linguistic counterpart of the Christian mission's rejection by the synagogue, and its subsequent turning to the Gentiles. It is not a point to be pressed but rather to be pondered. Much more solid is the contention that the primitive expectation of an imminent parousia would act as a deterrent to early Christian writing. It was not worthwhile to marry, to be manumitted or to change one's condition in any respect. Equally penetrating is the question raised regarding the occasion of the Apocalypse if a Semitic original be assumed. Since it is addressed to the Greek churches of Asia Minor, why would it have been written in Hebrew or Aramaic? In fact, there is no compelling reason for conjecturing an Aramaic literature even for a Jewish reading public. In his desire to make his case for the widespread use of Aramaic, Torrey neglected to mention that in the period after Alexander Greek was spoken in all places of the Western Diaspora of which we have any knowledge.

Similarly Goodspeed's view that the Gospels, Acts 1–15 and the Apocalypse *could* not have been written in Palestine was argued effectively. Underlying all his criticism was his conviction that the historical theological environment of first century Palestine was thoroughly non-literary. One of his last contributions to the debate opened with a citation from the Book of Enoch to the effect that it was the fourth of the fallen angels "who instructed mankind in writing with ink and paper, and thereby, many sinned from eternity to eternity and until this day. For men were not created for

---

[12] *New Chapters in New Testament Study*, 128.

such a purpose, to give confirmation to their good faith in pen and ink."[13] It would be difficult to put the wickedness of literary composition more bluntly. Yet, said Goodspeed, such was the Jewish point of view in the first century before Christ. Ralph Marcus pointed out in Goodspeed's favor that Torrey's explanation of the verbal and material variations in the synoptic parallels as the usual result of oral transmission, and the examples he gives of the power of memory and accuracy of ancient traditionaries, seem to support the position of those who hold that the undeniable Semitisms of the Gospels are owing to the evangelists' use of oral tradition in Hebrew or Aramaic rather than their use of documents in Hebrew or Aramaic.[14] Goodspeed's contention that the total absence of literary remains indicates that there was no Aramaic literature was not adequately answered by his opponents. Torrey and Olmstead might point to the Aramaic of coins and inscriptions, but so eminent an authority as W. F. Albright conceded that the majority of these contained but a name or two; and if they provided any insight into first century Palestinian Aramaic, it was not in Torrey's favor.

Finally, the disagreement among the Semitists in the identification of Semitisms and mistranslations became, in Goodspeed's hands, an effective weapon against their position. At the climax of the debate Torrey wrote:

> Our NT friends are perfectly right in holding retroversions and alleged mistranslations in deep suspicion (the field is not a playground for sophomores), but it is beyond question that the more serious slips of a translator *can* be recognized and shown conclusively—in any language. Such instances furnish the proof which is at once the most striking and the most reliable.[15]

This kind of statement was turned upon the Aramaic school with a vengeance by Goodspeed and his colleagues. New Testament scholars had been steadily declared to be incompetent to judge the Semitisms which were "obvious" to Semitic specialists alone. Nothing, therefore, strengthened Goodspeed's criticism of the method of the Aramaic school more than the spectacle of the Semitists rejecting each other's evidence in favor of their own "obvious" identifications.

The weakness in Goodspeed's position may be summed up in a single phrase: he overstated his case. If Torrey was obsessed with the idea that the primitive Palestinian church had produced a voluminous Aramaic literature within a generation of Jesus' death, Goodspeed seemed equally bent on denying that it had so much as made a few notes. At this point he parted company with many colleagues who were equally opposed to Torrey's central thesis, but who were willing to admit the probability of at least fragmentary written Aramaic sources. Similarly, if Torrey dated the Gospels

---

[13] "Greek Idiom in the Gospels," *JBL* 63 (1944) 87.
[14] "Notes on Torrey's Translation of the Gospels," *HTR* 27 (1934) 211–39.
[15] "The Aramaic of the Gospels," *JBL* 61 (1942) 82.

early, Goodspeed would go to any length to prove them late. Thus he interprets John 17:14, ὁ κόσμος ἐμίσησεν αὐτούς, as evidence pointing to the persecution under Nero and Domitian. Surely it is one thing to say that the persecutions under Nero and Domitian are examples of the hatred of the world for the disciples of Christ; but it is quite another to assume that such hatred *began* with these persecutions. The Fourth Gospel emphasizes that the world first hated Jesus and naturally continued to hate those who were his from the beginning. Again, if Scott or Torrey asserted that the Apocalypse of John was originally a Semitic document, Goodspeed was ready to discover Greek influence everywhere. He did not stop short of suggesting that the number of twenty-four elders reflects the chorus of the late Greek comedy. These elders have been variously taken as (1) glorified men, the number being the sum of the twelve patriarchs and the twelve apostles; (2) a college of angels, a conception borrowed from apocalyptic tradition influenced by the twenty-four star gods of Babylonia; (3) angelic representatives of the twenty-four priestly orders; and (4) representatives of the whole body of the faithful. It is very likely that Goodspeed was the first and last to derive their number from the chorus of Greek drama.

Because both Goodspeed and Torrey represented extreme positions, it cannot be said that either of them established his view. It may, however, be said that the priority of written Greek Gospels, so ardently championed by Goodspeed, as over against written Aramaic Gospels continues to hold sway. Today the Aramaic approach to the New Testament is represented by the work of Matthew Black. Torrey, he writes,

> bases his conclusions mainly on examples of mistranslation of Aramaic originals. Most of his examples of mistranslation, however, and several of Burney's, are open to grave objection. Torrey's attempt at a new translation of the Gospels before any adequate presentation of the philological evidence was premature. . . . Mistranslation of an original is, it is true, the best proof of translation; but it is doubtful if it can ever have scientific value as evidence except in cases where we possess not only the translation but also the original work.[16]

Black's own study of syntax, grammar, vocabulary, Semitic poetic form in the Gospels and evidence of mistranslation and interpretation in Aramaic, yields only one conclusion which can be regarded as in any degree established: that an Aramaic sayings source or tradition lies behind the synoptic Gospels. Whether that source was written or oral, cannot be determined from the evidence. Even where the evangelists are dependent upon Aramaic sources, the character of their "translation" is such that they are for the most

---

[16] *An Aramaic Approach to the Gospels and Acts* (3d ed.; Oxford: Clarendon Press, 1967) 5ff.

part writing Greek Gospels. This position, which commands the respect of contemporary New Testament scholarship, is manifestly closer to Goodspeed than to Torrey.

VI
A LIFE OF JESUS

The final decade of Goodspeed's literary activity was marked by an interest in biographical stories of major New Testament personalities. Inasmuch as Jesus of Nazareth is the central figure of the New Testament, it might be assumed that a writing of his life would be the natural climax to the labors of a New Testament specialist. The results of modern critical studies, however, have led scholars to become increasingly reluctant to make the attempt. Although Goodspeed did not detail his own position on this problem, the implication is that he wrote *A Life of Jesus*[1] in order to honor the request of his wife rather than out of a compelling desire on his part to make a contribution to this area of New Testament study. After describing the fatal illness of Mrs. Goodspeed in his autobiography, he continues:

> But with her departure I came suddenly to realize that all the joy in this world is the creation of these wonderful women, our wives and mothers. I could only throw myself into writing the book on the life of Christ she had so much wanted me to write and then devote its material profits to her memorial.[2]

Goodspeed gives some indication of his basically non-theological approach to the subject in the prefatory remarks of his life of Jesus that set forth in a general way why the story is important and what is basic to it. He acknowledges that while that story can never be written adequately, it must ever remain fresh in human memory "for its sheer influence on human thought, human relations and human destiny, and for its incomparable contribution to man's faith in good and goodness."[3] Of similar interest is the fact that Goodspeed regards emotion as the ingredient which is basic and central in the biography of Jesus: "For it is the record of great emotions—of commission, temptation, devotion, compassion, surrender, and sacrifice. If one is a stranger to these emotions, he can never penetrate to the meaning of Jesus' life and ministry, for he was a man of great emotions."[4] This statement is promptly qualified by the observation that, inasmuch as these emotions were also convictions, the stranger to convictions is equally helpless before the

---

[1] (New York: Harper & Brothers, 1950).
[2] *As I Remember* (New York: Harper & Brothers, 1953) 302.
[3] *A Life of Jesus* (New York: Harper & Brothers, 1950) 11.
[4] Ibid.

riddle of the personality of Jesus. The characterization of the latter's ministry as the most tremendous and paradoxical drama in human history is climaxed by the declaration that "Its apparent failure was its stupendous suc-
cess."[5]

Throughout the book, Goodspeed chose to hold the traditional Christian
identification of Jesus to a minimum. The idea of divine sonship before
Jesus' baptism was limited to the prophetic teaching that the members of
the chosen people were the sons of the living God. There appears to be some
advance made on this position at the baptism, when Jesus underwent the experience of being in a special sense the Son of God. Nevertheless, he was
distinguished from the prophets in function but not in being. Jesus' mighty
works declared him to be more than a teacher who pointed men to a better
way, but what more he was, or why, Goodspeed did not suggest. Similarly,
no definite examples of the Messianic sense of the "Son of Man" are offered.
Throughout the scattered references to Jesus' identity there is no mention of
the incarnation.

Goodspeed found the message of Jesus centered in his proclamation of
the kingdom of heaven, the reign of God on earth. As John the Baptist had
done before him, he declared that human beings must repent and prepare
for it. Nevertheless, Jesus' teaching about the kingdom differed from that of
John in two respects. First, "Jesus announced it not as doom but as good
news. He preached a gospel, in which men must believe. He invited them to
share in the joy and blessing of the kingdom he proclaimed. It was to bring
men happiness, not misery. He foresaw a fuller, better life for those who
would accept his message."[6] Second, instead of foretelling the coming of the
kingdom, Jesus "stepped right into the picture and began to set it up. He did
not predict it, he began it. He inaugurated it and undertook to carry out the
greatest task ever conceived—to set up the kingdom of God on earth."[7]
Jesus' role in the establishment of the kingdom, as described by Goodspeed,
was to be understood in terms of invitation and example. He invited people
"to welcome the spirit of God into their hearts and live in the assurance of
his forgiveness, his care and his love—yes, and of his presence too within
them."[8] The Sermon on the Mount ("a little gospel all by itself") "*told* Jesus'
hearers how to live in the kingdom of heaven; his own life of tireless useful-
ness *showed* them how to do it. He went about doing good."[9] He declared
the kingdom's program to be "self-help and mutual help,"[10] and its secret

---

[5] Ibid., 12.

[6] Ibid., 45–46.

[7] Ibid., 64.

[8] Ibid., 51.

[9] Ibid., 85.

[10] Ibid., 84.

was the "conception of religion which Pharisaic legalists would not permit him to proclaim to the people generally."[11]

Goodspeed thus portrayed the kingdom and its establishment in the most optimistic terms. There was no real need for Jesus to be more than the bearer of God's invitation. There was apparently no evil to be wrestled with and therefore Jesus' mission was not one of deliverance but of enlightenment. Sin was chiefly a matter of ignorance. Once people had been told and shown how God desired them to live, they too would go about doing good. In the absence of any real opposition, it was perfectly understandable that Jesus would be sure that his undertaking would succeed.

In Goodspeed's re-creation of the gospel story, the death of Jesus was the direct result of his clash with the institutional religion of Judaism. It is after Mark reports that the "Pharisees went out, and immediately held counsel with the Herodians against him, how to destroy him" (3:6), that Goodspeed first discerned the shadow of the cross. The so-called "Passion Sayings" of Mark's Gospel are noted as they occur in the narrative but generally without comment. In the midst of a chapter describing the relationship between Jesus and John the Baptist, Goodspeed suddenly inserted this one-sentence paragraph: "It is plain that Jesus feels that he is carrying out the role of the Suffering Servant of Isaiah's prophecy, not at all the traditional Jewish view of the Messiah."[12] Precisely what Goodspeed understood by these descriptions of Jesus' awareness of his approaching passion is difficult to determine, for Jesus is portrayed as hopeful to the end. As he moved on to Jerusalem with increasing danger from the Pharisee-Herodian alliance, he was not without hope of winning the Jewish people to his side:

> At their great annual feast he would present himself to them, wipe out the wrongs that oppressed them, and offer them their great Messianic destiny, the moral and religious leadership of mankind. They might accept it and indeed set up the kingdom of God on earth. It was his deepest hope that they would do so. But if they did not, and he must pay for his effort with his life, he would do so in a manner which should forever commemorate his great undertaking, and make his message remembered long after he was gone. He would create a memory that should be eternal. The proof of this is the historical fact that he did so! This was surely no accident.[13]

The same desire to be remembered motivated the transformation of the Passover into the Lord's Supper: Jesus meant it to be the vehicle for perpetuating his work and his memory. He also meant it "to weld them into a new society, based upon their assurance that his death was not the end of his work but the climax of it, as a great sacrifice to God on men's behalf, which

---

[11] Ibid., 100.
[12] Ibid., 111.
[13] Ibid., 134–35.

solemnized a new covenant between God and men."[14] In the light of all that has gone before, it is difficult to know what this last sentence means. It is obviously the most theological statement Goodspeed made about Jesus' death. At most it suggests that there may have been something more significant about the crucifixion than a simple execution, but inasmuch as the dominant purpose of the cross is described as the establishment of a memorial, it would be venturesome to find here a hint of a theory of the atonement.

With regard to the resurrection of Jesus, the predictions which in the Gospels are linked to the passion sayings were traced by Goodspeed to Hosea's words (6:1, 2):[15]

> Come, let us return to the Lord;
>> for he has torn, that he may heal us;
>> he has stricken, and he will bind us up.
> After two days he will revive us;
>> on the third day he will raise us up,
>> that we may live before him.

No mention is made of this in connection with the final prediction of Mark 14:28, however, for by this time the actual location of the rendezvous was definitely fixed in the mind of the disciples.

For the New Testament witness to the event of the resurrection, Goodspeed first refers to 1 Corinthians 15, noting that Paul apparently thought of the appearance to Peter as quite of the same kind as his own on the Damascus road. Continuing with the appearance to the eleven as recorded in Matthew 28, Goodspeed relates how in Galilee "they saw him and bowed down before him, though some were in doubt about it—a candid observation which in itself shows it was not a physical appearance."[16] These comments, together with the promise of the great commission, are then expanded into this interpretation:

> That he is to be with them always, to the very end, shows that it is not as a physical presence that he has come back to them, but as a spiritual one. As Dr. Buttrick once put it, "Their memory of him quickened to a presence!" The thing we most crave about our beloved departed is not so much their physical reanimation, but rather just this sense of their living presence with us, in our hearts, in guidance, sympathy, companionship and counsel. A physical presence if real could be in only one place at a time, but what the early church felt was Jesus' presence with every Christian heart, all over the ancient world.[17]

[14] Ibid., 200.
[15] Ibid., 125, 131.
[16] Ibid., 225.
[17] Ibid., 226.

In commenting on the crucifixion Goodspeed observed that for a little while the cruel death of Jesus must have seemed to his disciples the bitter, chilling end of all their hopes. "It is one of the paradoxes of history," he added, "indeed the chief such paradox, that it was just the opposite."[18] This statement appears to be a natural consequence of Goodspeed's view of the resurrection, a view which, significantly, makes no mention of the empty tomb. If the resurrection of Jesus does not differ in essence from a lively memory of "our beloved departed," the remarkable transformation of the disciples from despair to victory must indeed ever be the chief paradox of history.

In spite of the fact that critical problems are barely mentioned in *A Life of Jesus*, the book itself represents positions on several significant issues. Every attempt to write a life of Jesus in the twentieth century has had to take a position on the problem of the frame of the Gospels. This fact is largely owing to the investigations of D. W. Wrede and K. L. Schmidt. The former attacked the historicity of Mark's portrayal of Jesus' life in *The Messianic Secret*,[19] and the latter had concluded that "on the whole there is no life of Jesus in the sense of a developing life-story, no chronological pattern of the history of Jesus, but only individual stories, *pericopae*, which have been set in a framework."[20]

The significance of this result of form criticism for the writer of a life of Jesus was demonstrated by Martin Dibelius in his *Jesus*.[21] After agreeing with the earlier form critics that the events in the main period of Jesus' ministry are known to us only from narrative sections, he concluded:

> We are obliged therefore to forego chronological order from the outset, as well as the reconstruction of any development in Jesus, in his success, in his conflict with his enemies—a 'biography' of Jesus in this sense cannot be written. All we know is individual incidents, not interconnected events.[22]

The difference between this approach and that of Goodspeed is immediately apparent, even from the titles and tables of contents of the two books. Goodspeed is writing *A Life of Jesus*; Dibelius can speak simply of *Jesus*. Goodspeed's chapter headings (e.g., "Jesus Begins His Work in Galilee," "The First Clash With the Pharisees and the Choosing of the Twelve," "Advance Through Trans-Jordan") contain both chronological and geographical presuppositions. Dibelius, on the contrary, is completely topical: "People, Land, Descent," "The Movement Among the Masses," "The Opposing Forces." The difficulty with Goodspeed at this point is not that he evidently rejects the

---

[18] Ibid., 223.

[19] Trans. J. C. G. Greig (Cambridge: James Clarke & Co., 1971): "It must frankly be said that *Mark no longer has a real view of the historical life of Jesus*" (129).

[20] *Der Rahmen der Geschichte Jesu* (Berlin: Trowitzsh & Sohn, 1919) 317.

[21] Trans. C. B. Hedrick and F. C. Grant (Philadelphia: The Westminster Press, 1949).

[22] Ibid., 29.

results of form criticism, for many competent scholars have felt that the conclusions of Wrede and Schmidt are far too sweeping. It is rather that he writes this life of Jesus as if the researches of the form critics and the ensuing debate had never taken place. He had apparently arrived at some definite conclusions about this problem, and a scholar of his stature could be expected to explain the steps that brought him to them.

The length of Jesus' public ministry is a problem that has long exercised the skills of New Testament scholarship. In characteristic fashion, however, Goodspeed gave not the slightest hint that a problem was involved. The first mention of the matter is in the context of Gospel sources rather than chronology. He described the synoptic Gospels as the sources which bring us close to the Jesus of history, "in the few portentous months of his earthly ministry."[23] The basis for this statement is encountered in this later paragraph:

> Luke is the only one of our ancient sources to give us light on how the life and work of Jesus are to be fitted into the chronology of his times. Luke says that when Jesus began his work he was about thirty years of age (3:23). If John's work began in A.D. 28–29, the fifteenth year of the reign of Tiberius (Luke 3:1), and Jesus came to hear him soon after, say in the autumn, and John's arrest took place soon after Jesus' baptism, and Jesus began to preach soon after John's arrest, Jesus must have begun his work at the earliest toward the end of A.D. 28, and if he was born in 4 B.C. he would then be thirty-one or thirty-two. This would limit the time of his active ministry to little more than six months.[24]

This is a remarkably radical view of the Lukan or synoptic chronology.

If it is impossible to explain why Goodspeed chose to advance this view with such confidence, it may be possible to suggest how he arrived at it. He apparently assumed that Luke is the most chronologically reliable of the Gospels and then, by means of some unmentioned method of assigning time limits to specific events, drew the conclusion that the ministry there portrayed lasted only six months. There is no suggestion that Mark's evidence was considered at all, and of course the Johannine chronology was ignored completely. These factors, together with his rejection of the results of form criticism, enabled Goodspeed to fix the duration of the ministry with complete confidence.

In closely following the Markan order of events, Goodspeed inevitably came to the abrupt ending at Mark 16:8. Then, rather unexpectedly in a volume which up to this point has avoided any serious mention of critical problems, the life of Jesus is interrupted by a discussion of the fate of the "lost ending." After explaining how Mark's "complete absorption in the later and religiously superior Gospel of Matthew led to its disuse and neglect

---

[23] Ibid., 14.
[24] Ibid., 55.

until, when the four Gospels were collected and published, about 115–120, only a defective copy of Mark could be found for the purpose," he offered the assurance that, in fact, nothing has been lost:

> For the lost ending of Mark is unmistakably preserved for us in the closing paragraphs of the Gospel of Matthew. Matthew, we can see, is faithfully copying everything of significance in Mark; he has done so from the very first, so that we can actually find fifteen-sixteenths of all Mark says reproduced in Matthew. Should this be thought an exaggeration, we may remember that Canon Streeter said he found nineteen-twentieths of Mark in Matthew! But in these closing pages particularly, while Matthew has much to add, he is meticulously incorporating into his narrative all that Mark affords. From Matthew 27:1 on, except for four or five scattered verses, hardly a clause or even a phrase of Mark's account is left out by Matthew. And where our Mark breaks off, Matthew goes right on with the story Mark has been leading up to—the reunion with Jesus at their rendezvous in Galilee. This has been specifically anticipated twice in the Gospel of Mark.[25]

The scholarly status of this solution, whose correctness Goodspeed described as unmistakable, may be judged from the circumstance that the scant attention it has received has been negative.

A Life of Jesus is a fresh, crisp telling of the story of Jesus as Goodspeed had come to understand it. It was obviously intended to be an aid to the general reader's knowledge of Jesus' life and ministry rather than a contribution to the scientific investigation of the subject. In general, it is clear that Goodspeed preferred the Jesus of history to the Christ of dogma, a messianic mission of reformation to one of redemption, and the natural to the supernatural.

---

[25] Life, 244–45. It is difficult to avoid the impression that Goodspeed broke his critical silence here in order to advance once more a position he had urged on other occasions: see "The Original Conclusion of the Gospel of Mark," AJT 9 (1905) 484–90; "The Original Conclusion of Mark," Expositor, Ser. 8, 18 (1919) 155–60; An Introduction to the New Testament (Chicago: University of Chicago Press, 1937) 156.

EPILOGUE

By any standard of measurement Edgar J. Goodspeed made a sizable contribution to the area of biblical studies as a New Testament scholar. Destined for the life of a scholar from earliest years, he became an influential university professor and the author of more than fifty volumes. However critical his colleagues may have been of some of his positions, none ever questioned the soundness of his scholarship or the breadth of his learning. If Goodspeed did not exert a formative influence on New Testament thought in the sense of creating a "school," perhaps the reason is to be found in the fact that he was more of a New Testament technician than a New Testament theologian. At collating and deciphering manuscripts, wrestling with the problems of translation and formulating complex theories regarding the provenance of primitive Christian documents, Goodspeed was at his best. On the other hand, the only serious attempt made at exegesis or hermeneutics is found in the first part of *The Meaning of Ephesians*, and this is not so much a commentary as an attempt to demonstrate the validity of a specific hypothesis. While no advance in learning on any front is to be minimized, it must be acknowledged that it does not normally fall to the philologist, or even the translator, to deal with the ideas and beliefs that determine the lines of biblical thought.

This is not to say, however, that Goodspeed's impact, especially among American scholars, has been either slight or momentary. He was that most useful and practical of individuals, an articulate scholar. Enjoying a modest but successful reputation as a magazine essayist, Goodspeed prided himself on his ability to write the familiar spoken English of his day. He exercised this talent both in his translation of scripture and in his translation of advances in biblical science into the language of the laity.

While collecting materials on Goodspeed some years ago, the writer made the acquaintance of the woman who for twenty-six years served as the president of Spelman College, Atlanta, Georgia. Her own literary labors led her to make inquiry concerning the subject of my investigation. Upon learning that it was Edgar Goodspeed, she immediately described how much she had profited from a recent reading of his *The Story of the Bible*. The currency of such testimonials indicates that long after Goodspeed's learned contributions have taken their place in the history of research, men and women of many walks will continue to be instructed and, perhaps, inspired by the numerous volumes he addressed to them.

APPENDIX A

A CLASSIFIED LIST OF EDGAR J. GOODSPEED'S
BOOKS AND PAMPHLETS, WITH ANNOTATIONS

A. Palaeography and Papyrology

1. *Description of an Unedited Syriac Manuscript of the New Testament.* Chicago: 1897. Pp. 66.

   Typewritten thesis for the Bachelor of Divinity degree.

2. *Greek Papyri from the Cairo Museum, together with Papyri of Roman Egypt from American Collections.* Chicago: University of Chicago Press, 1902. Pp. 78.

   This volume is divided into three parts: I. Cairo Papyri: These fifteen papyri were transcribed during a visit to the Gizeh-Museum (now the Cairo Museum) made in the last months of 1899. II. The Alexander Papyri: These twelve papyri are from the collection made by the Reverend J. R. Alexander, of Asiut, Egypt, and deposited by him in the museum of Westminster College, New Wilmington, Penn. III. Chicago Papyri: These three papyri are from the editor's collection. These documents range in date from the third century B.C. to the fourth century A.D.

3. *Greek Gospel Texts in America.* Chicago: University of Chicago Press, 1902–18. Pp. ix, 186.

   The publications collected in this volume belong to the "Texts" series of the *Historical and Linguistic Studies in Literature Related to the New Testament,* issued from time to time by the Department of New Testament and Early Christian Literature of the University of Chicago. Included here are six collations of Greek Gospel manuscripts in American collections. They are: I. The Newberry Gospels; II. The Toronto Gospels; III. The Freer Gospels; IV. The Bixby Gospels; V. The Haskell Gospels; VI. The Harvard Gospels. Each manuscript is illustrated by a plate. The collation of the Newberry Gospels is the published form of Goodspeed's dissertation for the degree of Doctor of Philosophy at the University of Chicago.

4. *The Tebtunis Papyri* (with B. P. Grenfell and A. S. Hunt). London: H. Frowde, Oxford University Press, Part II, 1907. Pp. xv, 485.

   The volume deals with the papyri found in houses of the town during the first month of the excavations. With the exception of a few Ptolemaic documents these texts belong to the first three centuries of the Christian era. In the summer of 1900, while Grenfell and Hunt were occupied with other work, these papyri were studied by E. J. Goodspeed, who deciphered part of those included in the present volume and who was therefore associated with Grenfell and Hunt in their publication. Goodspeed also prepared the bulk of the indices. The decipherment of the rest of the texts was done by Grenfell and Hunt. A double map and facsimiles are included.

5.   *Chicago Literary Papyri*. Chicago: University of Chicago Press, 1908. Pp. viii, 50.

6.   A *Descriptive Catalogue of Manuscripts in the Libraries of the University of Chicago* (with Martin Sprengling). Chicago: University of Chicago Press, 1912. Pp. xi, 128.

This Catalogue, published in connection with the dedication of Harper Memorial Library, is the result of the conviction of the editors that the possession of manuscripts of even a moderate antiquity carries with it the responsibility of publishing some account of them for the use of scholars. Not all the manuscript holdings of the University at the time are included; those represented are in a variety of languages, including Latin, Greek, Italian, Spanish, French, German and English. The frontispiece illustrates The Haskell Gospels.

7.   *Untersuchungen über einige Papyrusfragmente einer griechischen Dichtung* (with David Meuli). Zürich: 1920. Pp. iii, 42.

This is a Zürich dissertation done by Meuli.

8.   *The Rockefeller McCormick New Testament* (with Donald W. Riddle and Harold R. Willoughby). 3 vols., Chicago: University of Chicago Press, 1932.

Goodspeed discovered this manuscript in a Paris antique shop in 1927. He was impressed by the splendor of the covers and frontispiece, the extent of the text, the beauty of the hand and above all by the wealth of its miniatures. With the help of his colleagues, Riddle and Willoughby, the manuscript was dated A.D. 1265–69. Mrs. Rockefeller McCormick authorized the purchase of the manuscript and it was brought to Chicago in 1928 and turned over to the Department of New Testament and Early Christian Literature of the University of Chicago. Riddle prepared the volume on the text (Volume II) and Willoughby the volume on the iconography (Volume III). Goodspeed wrote the Introduction, which, together with the color facsimile of the manuscript, constitutes Volume I.

9. *A Greek Papyrus Reader with Vocabulary* (with E. C. Colwell). Chicago: University of Chicago Press, 1935. Pp. 108.

This handbook was produced to give the student a selection of papyri texts, with a view to the light they may throw upon New Testament vocabulary, syntax, and style. For practice in translation the texts are accompanied by a concise vocabulary rather than English translations. The eighty-two papyri are reproduced unchanged from the editions from which they are taken, except that abbreviations are regularly expanded and punctuation, breathings and accents are supplied where the editors did not supply them. No effort is made to establish the ultimate text of these papyri. A brief description accompanies each document. The frontispiece illustrates a papyrus dated A.D. 143.

B. Patristics

10. *The Book of Thekla.* Chicago: University of Chicago Press, 1901. Pp. 35.

This edition of the Ethiopic text of the Book of Thekla, as preserved in two codices (Brit. Mus. Orient. 689 and 687–688), is one of the fascicles in *Historical and Linguistic Studies in Literature Related to the New Testament*, issued by the Department of Biblical and Patristic Greek of the University of Chicago. The Ethiopic text is followed by an English translation.

11. *The Martyrdom of Cyprian and Justa.* Chicago: University of Chicago Press, 1903. Pp. 22.

This edition of the Ethiopic text of the Martyrdom of Cyprian and Justa, as preserved in three manuscripts (Brit. Mus. Orient. 689; 687–688), is one of the fascicles in *Historical and Linguistic Studies in Literature Related to the New Testament*, issued by the Department of Biblical and Patristic Greek of the University of Chicago. The Ethiopic text is followed by an English translation.

12. *Ancient Sermons for Modern Times, by Asterius, Bishop of Amasia* (with Galhusha Anderson). New York: Pilgrim Press, 1904. Pp. 157.

13. *Index Patristicus, sive Clavis Patrum Apostolicorum Operum.* Leipzig: J. C. Hinrichs, 1907. Pp. viii, 262.

This volume utilizes the small editions of Gebhardt, Harnack, and Zahn, with readings from the small editions of Funk and Lightfoot. It is designed to serve the purpose of a concordance to the early patristic literature. The words and the forms of the Greek texts of the Apostolic Fathers are exhaustively covered by this index. The work is modeled after the Index Homericus of August Gehring. Goodspeed was assisted in the preparation of this work by a number of students.

14. *The Conflict of Severus, Patriarch of Antioch, by Athanasius* (with the remains of the Coptic Versions ed. and trans. W. E. Crum). *Patrologia Orientalis,* Vol. IV, Paris: Firmin-Didot, 1908. Pp. 569–726.

This is an edition and translation of the Ethiopic version as preserved in two manuscripts (Brit. Mus. Orient. 773 and 771), and in part in one manuscript, numbered 31, in the D'Abbadie collection. Goodspeed concludes that the immediate parent of the Ethiopic was an Arabic version.

15. *Index Apologeticus, sive Clavis Iustini Martyris Operum Aliorumque Apologetarum Pristinorum.* Leipzig: J. C. Hinrichs, 1912. Pp. vi, 300.

This Index to the writings of the Apologists attempts to accomplish for this portion of pre-Catholic literature what the *Index Patristicus* did for that part. The year A.D. 180 is the *terminus ad quem* which determines the documents to be considered. Goodspeed was aided in the preparation of the Index by four of his students. The work is based upon the best texts available and has the additional feature of including the variant readings of the chief manuscripts.

16. *Die älteste Apologeten; Texte mit kurzen Einleitung.* Göttingen: Vandenhoeck & Ruprecht, 1914. Pp. xi, 380.

Goodspeed prepared this volume in the belief that a manual edition of the oldest Apologists offering a reliable Greek text with a limited selection of readings would meet a long felt need. Works included are limited to those prior to Irenaeus; and of texts not covered by the *Index Apologeticus,* the only one here admitted is the non-Eusebian fragment of Melito. Citations and echoes of biblical or classical literature are marked by underlining.

17. *The Epistle of Pelagia.* Chicago: University of Chicago Press, 1931. Pp. 14.

This edition of the Ethiopic text of the Epistle of Pelagia as preserved in three manuscripts (Brit. Mus. Orient. 686; 687–688; and 689) is a fascicle in *Historical and Linguistic Studies in Literature Related to the New Testament,* issued by the Department of Biblical and Patristic Greek of the University of Chicago. The Ethiopic text is followed by an English translation.

18. *The Story of Eugenia and Philip.* Chicago: University of Chicago Press, 1931. Pp. 21.

This edition of the Ethiopic text of the Story of Eugenia and Philip, as preserved in three manuscripts (Brit. Mus. Orient. 686; 687–688; and 689), is a fascicle in *Historical and Linguistic Studies in Literature Related to the New Testament,* issued by the Department of Biblical and Patristic Greek of the University of Chicago. The Ethiopic text is followed by an English translation.

19. *A History of Early Christian Literature.* Chicago: University of Chicago Press, 1942. Pp. xiii, 324.

This volume emphasizes that the New Testament was really the bursting-forth of a great literary movement whose first literary models and patterns were found in the sermons, letters, revelations, gospels and acts of the New Testament. The development of this literature is traced from the writings of the Apostolic Fathers to Arnobius, Lactantius and other Latin authors just prior to the Council of Nicea. During that period of early Christian literature which can be described as a conscious literary movement, a strict order of treatment by chronology or literary type is rejected in favor of presenting the work of each author as a unit in relation to his times and problems.

20. *The Apostolic Fathers, An American Translation.* New York: Harper & Brothers, 1950. Pp. xi, 321.

Goodspeed notes that the canon of the Apostolic Fathers has varied greatly in the various editions. He ventures beyond his predecessors and includes the Doctrina, the Greek Barnabas, as well as most of the later documents that have long been regarded as reproducing material from the Greek Didache. The translation is based on the Funk-Bihlmeyer edition, vol. 1 (Tübingen, 1924), except for the Shepherd of Hermas, which Goodspeed translated from Lake's edition in the Loeb Library (1913), with occasional emendations derived from the papyri. Each document is preceded by a brief introduction discussing its provenance.

C. New Testament Introduction

21. *Harmony of the Four Gospels in the Latin Vulgate.* Chicago: n. d. Pp. 2, 7, 120.

Partial transcription by E. J. Goodspeed

22. *A Harmony of the Synoptic Gospels for Historical and Critical Study* (with Ernest DeWitt Burton). New York: Charles Scribner's Sons, 1917. Pp. xv, 275.

This volume is intended to bring the *Harmony of the Four Gospels* prepared by William Arnold Stevens and Ernest DeWitt Burton (1894) in line with subsequent research on the synoptic problem. The Fourth Gospel is not included because (1) it is a product of a time later than that in which the synoptic gospels were produced and of a different kind of literary process, and (2) the first three gospels are related to one another by an intimate genealogical connection. This harmony attempts to set the English text of the first three gospels in such parallelism as will make the facts themselves tell their own story. The text employed is that of the American Standard Version (1901). The order of Mark is followed in all sections found in that Gospel.

23. *A Harmony of the Synoptic Gospels in Greek* (with Ernest DeWitt Burton). Chicago: University of Chicago Press, 1920. Pp. xxx, 316.

Except for the language, this work is in method and execution substantially identical with that of *A Harmony of the Synoptic Gospels for Historical and Critical Study* (1917). The Greek text employed is that of Westcott and Hort.

24. *The Formation of the New Testament.* Chicago: University of Chicago Press, 1926. Pp. ix, 209.

This volume traces the emergence of the canon from the standpoint of collections rather than individual books and assigns the making of these collections to such centers as Ephesus, Rome, Alexandria, and Antioch. In addition to the history of the canon, there are chapters on the Age of the Councils, the Middle Ages, the Age of Printing, the New Testament Apocrypha and the New Testament today.

25. *New Solutions of New Testament Problems.* Chicago: University of Chicago Press, 1927. Pp. xi, 127.

Goodspeed contended that Christian literature developed by collections rather than by individual documents. The purpose of this volume is to present this position and to offer some substantiation for it. Chapters six through ten are reprinted, with some revisions, from articles in the *Expositor* and the *Journal of Biblical Literature*.

26. *The Student's Gospels: A Harmony of the Synoptics, The Gospel of John* (with Shailer Matthews). Chicago: University of Chicago Press, 1927. Pp. ix, 193. 2d ed., 1934. Pp. xiv, 252.

27. *The Meaning of Ephesians.* Chicago: University of Chicago Press, 1933. Pp. viii, 170.

Part I is a presentation of Goodspeed's hypothesis concerning the occasion and purpose of Ephesians, together with an interpretation of the letter in the light of this hypothesis. Part II presents the continuous text of Ephesians in Greek with part of Colossians and other letters of Paul printed in parallel columns to show resemblances.

28. *An Introduction to the New Testament.* Chicago: University of Chicago Press, 1937. Pp. xvii, 362.

This volume reflects Goodspeed's view on a new organization of New Testament Introduction. This view is that once the significance of the Pauline letter collection is properly understood, it at once organizes the whole New Testament material into the works written before that event, and the ones that were written after it and under the influence or imitation of the newly published collection. The arrangement accordingly presents the Pauline letters first, followed by Mark, Matthew, and the work of Luke. Then the collection of the Pauline letters is discussed, followed by the rest of the New Testament literature.

29. *New Chapters in New Testament Study.* New York: The Macmillan Company, 1937. Pp. viii, 223.

This volume constitutes the Ayer lectures for 1937, delivered by Goodspeed under the auspices of the Colgate-Rochester Divinity School, with the addition of four chapters. Topics dealt with include the publication of early Christian literature, New Testament translation, pseudonymity and pseudepigraphy in early Christian literature and modern apocrypha. Each chapter is complete in itself.

30. *Christianity Goes to Press.* New York: The Macmillan Company, 1940. Pp. 115.

This book is based upon the James W. Richard lectures delivered by the author at the University of Virginia in 1939. It presents his hypothesis on the role that the collection and publishing of Paul's letters played in the production and form of the New Testament literature. The final chapter concerns the history of Bible publication in ancient and modern times.

31. *The Key to Ephesians.* Chicago: University of Chicago Press, 1956. Pp. xvi, 75.

This volume repeats the Ephesian hypothesis formulated by Goodspeed with the added conjecture that the writer of the letter is

Onesimus. Part II is the documentary evidence of *The Meaning of Ephesians* (1933) in English translation.

D. Translation

32. *The New Testament, An American Translation.* Chicago: University of Chicago Press, 1923. Pp. ix, 481.

This is Goodspeed's rendering of the New Testament into vernacular, American English, with a format to match. In appearance it resembles any other book. With the few exceptions noted in the Preface of the work, the translation is based upon the Greek text of Westcott and Hort.

33. *The Making of the English New Testament.* Chicago: University of Chicago Press, 1925. Pp. ix, 129.

A review of the story of the English New Testament. The combination of widespread public interest and ignorance of the history of the English New Testament which Goodspeed encountered at the publication of his own translation motivated him to chronicle the progress in New Testament studies which paralleled the great advances in the fields of industry, communication, transportation, medicine and science. The story is related with special emphasis on modern text discoveries, the significance of the Greek papyri and the advent of modern speech translations.

34. *The Synoptic Gospels: Matthew, Mark, Luke: An American Translation.* Chicago: University of Chicago Press, 1930. Pp. iv, 172.

35. *The Bible: An American Translation.* (The Old Testament translation by a group of scholars under the editorship of J. M. P. Smith). Chicago: University of Chicago Press, 1931. Pp. xvii, 1619, iv, 418.

The translators present their work as a new translation of the Bible based upon the assured results of modern study and put in the familiar language of today.

36. *The Short Bible: An American Translation.* (with J. M. P. Smith). Chicago: University of Chicago Press, 1933. Pp. x, 545.

This volume is intended to introduce the reader to the development of Hebrew and Christian religious thought. It is based upon the translation work of J. M. P. Smith and Goodspeed. The books selected for inclusion are arranged in the probable order of their production and each is prefaced with a brief account of its origin and purpose. The death of Smith before the work was finished left Goodspeed with the task of recasting the form of the introductions to the Old Testament books as well as the decisions about the order in which the books are arranged.

37. *The Translators to the Reader; Preface to the King James Version, 1611.* Chicago: University of Chicago Press, 1935. Pp. 38.

The first part of this booklet consists of "The Translators to the Reader," an essay by Goodspeed revised from his article of the same title in *Religion and Life,* I (1932). It is a plea for the inclusion of the original great Preface in all printings of the King James Bible so that the public can be informed about the facts as to its origin and ancestry. The plea is substantiated by several examples of misconceptions about that version. The second and third parts consist of a reprint, with spellings modernized, and a facsimile reproduction of the "Translators to the Reader," from the Hoe copy of the 1611 edition of the King James Version.

38. *The Junior Bible: An American Translation* (Illustrated by F. Dobias). New York: The Macmillan Company, 1936. Pp. xii, 282.

This volume gathers the parts of the Bible that are of most interest to young people from ten to fifteen years of age. The text used is the American translation. To help the reader to understand the stories and speeches, a brief introduction has been provided for each section.

39. *The Apocrypha, An American Translation.* Chicago: University of Chicago Press, 1938. Pp. ix, 493.

A lucid English rendering of the fourteen books constituting the Old Testament Apocrypha. Each book is preceded by a brief introduction providing information on provenance. The translation is essentially based on the critical Greek text of the Septuagint, edited by Alfred Rahlfs. Except for the Latin II Esdras, the translation is based directly on the Greek text.

40. *The Complete Bible: An American Translation* (The Old Testament translation is by J. M. P. Smith and a group of scholars). Chicago: University of Chicago Press, 1939. Pp. xvi, 883, iv, 202, iv, 247.

This edition emphasizes Goodspeed's contention that historically and culturally, the books of the Apocrypha are an integral part of the Bible. The Goodspeed translation of the Apocrypha is accordingly included in this edition.

41. *The Parallel New Testament, The American Translation and the King James Version in Parallel Columns.* Chicago: University of Chicago Press, 1943. Pp. viii, 600.

This book answers the question: How does a modern translation, embodying the advances in biblical scholarship, compare, verse by verse, with the King James? The King James text used is that of the American Bible Society.

42. *Problems of New Testament Translation.* Chicago: University of Chicago Press, 1945. Pp. xix, 215.

Goodspeed presents more than one hundred New Testament passages which offer peculiar difficulty to the translator. In each instance he states where the traditional readings of the King James and revised versions originated; how modern translators dealt with them in the private translations of the previous decades; and finally, what new light has been thrown upon them by the Greek papyri, the Greek inscriptions, wider study of Greek literature and recent lexical and grammatical studies. In effect, Goodspeed details the translation process that stands behind the renderings of these passages in his American translation.

43. *The Student's New Testament: The Greek Text and the American Translation.* Chicago: University of Chicago Press, 1954. Pp. x, 1055.

This volume presents the Greek text of Westcott and Hort in parallel columns with his American translation.

E. Biographies of New Testament Personalities

44. *Paul.* Philadelphia: J. C. Winston Co., 1947. Pp. ix, 246.

A recounting of the life of Paul from his boyhood in Tarsus to his probable martyrdom in Rome. Goodspeed views the method of a Pauline biographer to be that of weaving the letters into the narrative of the Acts as the weaver weaves his threads into the warp on his loom. The style is popular. The author's hypothesis of the origin of the Pauline corpus is presented in the final chapter, "The Return of Paul."

45. *A Life of Jesus.* New York: Harper & Brothers, 1950. Pp. 248.

A readable narrative of the life and ministry of Jesus as Goodspeed had come to understand them. The Markan order of events is followed. Luke and Matthew are also utilized as sources, but the Fourth Gospel is excluded as supplying no reliable historical data.

46. *The Twelve, the Story of Christ's Apostles.* Philadelphia: J. C. Winston Co., 1957. Pp. 182.

A book which attempts to do for the twelve apostles what the author had earlier done for Paul. Believing that, although we possess little factual material about the apostles, what Christian tradition made out of them is both significant and important, Goodspeed included much that was done and written in their names by a loyal and devout posterity.

47. *Matthew, Apostle and Evangelist.* Philadelphia: J. C. Winston, 1959. Pp. ix, 166.

A defense of the tradition which assigns the authorship of the first gospel to the apostle Matthew. The argument hinges upon the contention that, following the example of Isaiah, Jesus specifically called Matthew to exercise his record keeping abilities as a tax collector in the service of recording his teaching. When the Gospel of Mark appeared, Matthew decided to perfect it by supplementing its record of events with his own materials concerning Jesus' teaching. Matthew artfully but decisively reveals his hand in his highly mathematical treatment of the genealogy, for example, whose three groups of fourteen (or six groups of seven) reveal him to be a statistician and worker with figures. The reconstruction offered here is in marked contrast to Goodspeed's position held in earlier works.

F. Popular Bible Study Helps

48. *The Epistle to the Hebrews.* New York: Macmillan, 1908. Pp. xi, 132.

Goodspeed contributed this volume to the series, *The Bible for Home and School,* which was under the general editorship of Shailer Matthews. It conforms to the series in its rigid exclusion of all processes, both critical and exegetical, from its notes; its presuppositions and its use of the assured results of historical investigation and criticism; its running analysis both in text and comment; its brief explanatory notes; and its use of the Revised Version of 1881 as its text. It is intended for the intelligent Sunday School teacher, clergy and other lay readers.

49. *The Story of the New Testament.* Boston: Beacon Press, 1916. Pp. xi, 150; Chicago: University of Chicago Press, 2d ed., 1929. Pp. xiv, 150; Chinese trans. by Timothy Jen, Shanghai: Chinese Christian Literature Association, 1927. Pp. 156.

A brief introduction to the New Testament literature written for intelligent laypersons and young people. It is designed both as a study book for individual and group use, or for a continuous reading of the story as the title implies. Study suggestions are provided. The book represents Goodspeed's views before he had developed his later theories regarding Ephesians and the Pauline Corpus and their subsequent influence on New Testament literature.

50. *The Gospel of John.* Chicago: University of Chicago Press, 1917. Pp. 43.

This booklet is one of a series of *Outline Bible-Study Courses* issued by the American Institute of Sacred Literature, the University of Chicago. It was to serve as a correspondence course textbook for non-resident biblical and religious study. It describes the Fourth Gospel as originating in the early second century at Ephesus in order to relate the gospel to the contemporary religious thought. The material is grouped into a five-month study period.

51. *The Story of the Old Testament.* Chicago: University of Chicago Press, 1934. Pp. xii, 181.

A guide and introduction to the reading and study of the Old Testament. The books are arranged in the general order of their composition, beginning with Amos. The results of current Old Testament critical study are incorporated. Brief chapters on the formation of the Old Testament and the Apocryphal books are included.

52. *The Story of the Bible.* Chicago: University of Chicago Press, 1936. Pp. xvi, 187; iv, 150.

This volume is a reprinting of *The Story of the Old Testament* (1934) and *The Story of the New Testament* (1916) as one book.

53. *The Story of the Apocrypha.* Chicago: University of Chicago Press, 1939. Pp. ix, 150.

A concise introduction to the books of the Old Testament Apocrypha. In addition to the treatment of the individual books, there are chapters dealing with the Apocrypha in the Bible, the New Testament and the Christian Church. The book is intended for the student and the general reader.

54. *How Came the Bible.* New York: Abingdon-Cokesbury Press, 1940. Pp. 148.

This volume gathers up a series of thirteen lessons on the formation, transmission, and translation of the Bible which originally appeared in the autumn issues of *The Adult Bible Class Monthly* (1940) under the title, "The Growth of the Bible." No attempt is made to tell how the several books of the Bible came to be written, but only how, once written, they came to be gathered into the Old and New Testaments and the Apocrypha, and how these came down across the centuries to modern times. Questions are provided following each chapter.

55. *How to Read the Bible.* Philadelphia: Universal Book and Bible House, 1946. Pp. 256.

   A volume intended as a companion to Bible reading. It follows a literary and historical approach to the Bible, taking up the chief books in it as biography, oratory, history, poetry, drama, fiction, letters and visions, in the light of the times that produced them and the purposes of their writers. Books of the Old Testament Apocrypha are included, and a chapter on English Bibles concludes the book.

G. Miscellaneous Books and Pamphlets

56. *The Student's Handbook* (with Theodore G. Soares). Chicago: University of Chicago Press, 1893. Pp. 84.

57. *Homeric Vocabularies: Greek and English Word-Lists for the Study of Homer* (with William B. Owen). Chicago: University of Chicago Press, 1906. 2d ed., 1909. Pp. viii, 62.

58. *The University of Chicago in 1921.* Chicago: University of Chicago Press, 1921. Pp. 32.

59. *Things Seen and Heard.* Chicago: University of Chicago Press, 1925. Pp. ix, 226.

   A collection of essays on various subjects, the title of the book being taken from the first piece. Six of the papers also appeared in the *Atlantic Monthly,* and one in the *Chicago Herald.* Some reflect Goodspeed's academic environment, but they are literary compositions rather than New Testament studies.

60. *The University of Chicago Chapel: A Guide.* Chicago: University of Chicago Press, 1928. Pp. xi, 66.

   An account of the building prepared at the suggestion of the University administration. Eight illustrations of the chapel are included.

61. Goodspeed, Thomas W., *William Rainey Harper.* Chicago: University of Chicago Press, 1928. Pp. xi, 242.

   This volume was revised and completed after the author's death, by his sons, Charles T. B. Goodspeed and E. J. Goodspeed. Their contribution consisted in the revision of the first draft of the earlier chapters, the completion of the fifth chapter and the preparation of the sixth chapter.

62. *Strange New Gospels.* Chicago: University of Chicago Press, 1931. Pp. xi, 111.

A study of documents claiming to be genuine writings of Christian antiquity. Goodspeed describes their origin and contents and exposes their fraudulent character by subjecting them to the methods of modern historical criticism.

63. *Buying Happiness.* Chicago: University of Chicago Press, 1932. Pp. x, 191.

64. *The University Chapel.* Chicago: University of Chicago Press, 1933. Pp. iv, 16.

65. *The Curse in the Colophon.* Chicago: Willett, Clark, & Company, 1935. Pp. 259.

The Rockefeller McCormick manuscript of the New Testament contains a colophon invoking the curse of the three hundred and eighteen holy fathers who assembled in Nicea upon anyone who should ever steal the book from the church or convent where it belonged. This novel was written in response to Mrs. Goodspeed's suggestion that her husband write a mystery story about the colophon. It is the tale of a treasure hunt which followed the deciphering of a mysterious curse in the colophon of a famous manuscript.

66. *The Four Pillars of Democracy.* New York: Harper & Brothers, 1940. Pp. 148.

Goodspeed's four pillars are faith in science, humanism, society and religion. One chapter is devoted to each of these constructive forces in human life, followed by a synthesis in which the interrelations of the four are described.

67. *As I Remember.* New York: Harper & Brothers, 1953. Pp. 315.

When Goodspeed published this autobiography he was an octogenarian whose professional experience had spanned the first half of the twentieth century. In addition to providing many details of an interesting life, the volume contains personal recollections of many prominent people of the time, the founding of the University of Chicago, the public reaction to the publication of *The New Testament, An American Translation* (1923), and the adventure and rewards of manuscript hunting.

68. *Modern Apocrypha.* Boston: Beacon Press, 1956. Pp. 124.

An assembling and bringing up to date of the texts the author had earlier discussed in *Strange New Gospels* (1931) and *New Chapters in New Testament Study* (1937), with some additional documents of very recent origin.

APPENDIX B

A LIST OF THE PUBLICATIONS OF
EDGAR J. GOODSPEED*

BOOKS

Harmony of the Four Gospels in the Latin Vulgate (partial transcription by Edgar J. Goodspeed) (Chicago, n.d.) 2, 7, 120

Description of an Unedited Syriac Manuscript of the New Testament (typewritten) (Chicago, 1897; thesis, D. B.) 66

The Book of Thekla ("Historical and Linguistic Studies," Ser. I, Vol. I, Part 1) (Chicago: University of Chicago Press, 1901) 35

Greek Papyri from the Cairo Museum, Together with Papyri of Roman Egypt from American Collections (Chicago: University of Chicago Press, 1902) i, 78

The Newberry Gospels ("Historical and Linguistic Studies," Ser. I, Vol. II, Part 1) (Chicago: University of Chicago Press, 1902; thesis, Ph.D.) 29

The Martyrdom of Cyprian and Justa ("Historical and Linguistic Studies," Ser. I, Vol. I, Part 2) (Chicago: University of Chicago Press, 1903) 22

Index patristicus: Sive clavis patrum apostolicorum operum (Leipzig: J. C. Hinrichs, 1907) viii, 262

Chicago Literary Papyri (Chicago: University of Chicago Press, 1908) viii, 50

The Epistle to the Hebrews ("The Bible for Home and School") (New York: Macmillan, 1908) xi, 132

The Toronto Gospels ("Historical and Linguistic Studies," Ser. I, Vol. II, Part 2) (Chicago: University of Chicago Press, 1911) 21

Index apologeticus: Sive clavis Iustini Martyris operum aliorumque apologetarum pristinorum (Leipzig: J. C. Hinrichs, 1912) vi, 300

The Freer Gospels ("Historical and Linguistic Studies," Ser. I, Vol. II, Part 3) (Chicago: University of Chicago Press, 1914) 65

Die ältesten Apologeten (Göttingen: Vandenhoeck & Ruprecht, 1914) xi, 380

The Bixby Gospels ("Historical and Linguistic Studies," Ser. I, Vol. II, Part 4) (Chicago: University of Chicago Press, 1915) 34

The Story of the New Testament (Boston: Beacon Press, 1916) xi, 150

The Story of the New Testament (Chicago: University of Chicago Press, 1916) xiv, 150 (2d ed. 1929)

The Gospel of John: An Outline Bible-Study Course of the American Institute of Sacred Literature (Chicago: University of Chicago Press, 1917) vi, 43

The Haskell Gospels ("Historical and Linguistic Studies," Ser. I, Vol. II, Part 5) (Chicago: University of Chicago Press, 1918) 16

The Harvard Gospels ("Historical and Linguistic Studies," Ser. I, Vol. II, Part 6) (Chicago: University of Chicago Press, 1918) 18

Greek Gospel Texts in America (see *The Newberry Gospels, The Toronto Gospels, The Freer Gospels, The Bixby Gospels, The Haskell Gospels,* and *The Harvard Gospels*) (Chicago: University of Chicago Press, 1902–18) ix, 186

The University of Chicago in 1921 (Chicago: University of Chicago Press, 1921) 32

---

* This list includes and extends the titles in James H. Cobb and Louis B. Jennings, *A Biography and Bibliography of Edgar Johnson Goodspeed* (Chicago: University of Chicago Press, 1948).

Paul: An Outline Bible-Study Course of the American Institute of Sacred Literature (Chicago: University of Chicago Press, 1922) v, 78

The New Testament: An American Translation (Chicago: University of Chicago Press, 1923) xi, 481

The Making of the English New Testament (Chicago: University of Chicago Press, 1925) ix, 129

Things Seen and Heard (Chicago: University of Chicago Press, 1925) ix, 226

The Formation of the New Testament (Chicago: University of Chicago Press, 1926) ix, 210

The Story of the New Testament (Chinese trans. Timothy Jen) (Shanghai: Chinese Christian Literature Association, 1927) 156

New Solutions of New Testament Problems (Chicago: University of Chicago Press, 1927) xi, 127

The University of Chicago Chapel: A Guide (Chicago: University of Chicago Press, 1928) xii, 66

The Synoptic Gospels: Matthew, Mark, Luke: An American Translation (Chicago: University of Chicago Press, 1930) iv, 172

Strange New Gospels (Chicago: University of Chicago Press, 1931) xi, 111

The Story of Eugenia and Philip ("Historical and Linguistic Studies," Ser. I, Vol. I, Part 3) (Chicago: University of Chicago Press, 1931) ii, 21

The Epistle of Pelagia ("Historical and Linguistic Studies," Ser. I, Vol. I, Part 4) (Chicago: University of Chicago Press, 1931) ii, 114

Ethiopic Martyrdoms ("Historical and Linguistic Studies," Ser. I, Vol. I) (Chicago: University of Chicago Press, 1931) viii, 102

Buying Happiness (Chicago: University of Chicago Press, 1932) x, 191

The Meaning of Ephesians (Chicago: University of Chicago Press, 1933) viii, 170

The University Chapel (Chicago: University of Chicago Press, 1933) iv, 16

The Story of the Old Testament (Chicago: University of Chicago Press, 1934) xii, 187

The Translators to the Reader: Preface to the King James Version 1611 (Chicago: University of Chicago Press, 1935) 4, 38, 12

The Curse in the Colophon (Chicago: Willett, Clark & Co., 1935) iii, 259

The Story of the Bible (Chicago: University of Chicago Press, 1936) xvi, 187, iv, 150

The Junior Bible: An American Translation (illustrated by Frank Dobias) (New York: Macmillan, 1936) xii, 282

An Introduction to the New Testament (Chicago: University of Chicago Press, 1937) xviii, 362

New Chapters in New Testament Study (New York: Macmillan, 1937) viii, 223

The Apocrypha: An American Translation (Chicago: University of Chicago Press, 1938) x, 493

The Story of the Apocrypha (Chicago: University of Chicago Press, 1939) x, 150

Christianity Goes to Press (New York: Macmillan, 1940) v, 115

The Four Pillars of Democracy (New York: Harper & Bros., 1940) v, 148

How Came the Bible? (New York: Abingdon-Cokesbury Press, 1940) 148

A History of Early Christian Literature (Chicago: University of Chicago Press, 1942) xiii, 324

The Goodspeed Parallel New Testament (Chicago: University of Chicago Press, 1943) viii, 600

Problems of New Testament Translation (Chicago: University of Chicago Press, 1945) xix, 215

How to Read the Bible (Philadelphia: John C. Winston Co., 1946) 256

Paul (Philadelphia: John C. Winston Co., 1947) ix, 246

A Life of Jesus (New York: Harper & Bros., 1950) 248

The Apostolic Fathers, An American Translation (New York: Harper & Bros., 1950) xi, 321

As I Remember (New York: Harper & Bros., 1953) 315

The Student's New Testament: The Greek Text and the American Translation (Chicago: University of Chicago Press, 1954) x, 1055

The Key to Ephesians (Chicago: University of Chicago Press, 1956) xvi, 75

Modern Apocrypha (Boston: Beacon Press, 1956) 124

The Twelve, The Story of Christ's Apostles (Philadelphia: J. C. Winston, 1957) 182
Matthew, Apostle and Evangelist (Philadelphia: J. C. Winston, 1959) ix, 166

COLLABORATIVE WORKS

With Theodore Gerald Soares, *The Student's Handbook* (issued by the Y.M.C.A. of the University of Chicago) (Chicago: University of Chicago Press, 1893) 64

With Galusha Anderson, *Ancient Sermons for Modern Times, by Asterius, Bishop of Amasia* (New York: Pilgrim Press, 1904) 157

With William Bishop Owen, *Homeric Vocabularies: Greek and English Word-Lists for the Study of Homer* (Chicago: University of Chicago Press, 1906; 2d ed. 1909) viii, 62

With Bernard P. Grenfell and Arthur S. Hunt, *The Tebtunis Papyri*, Part II (London: Henry Frowde, 1907) xv, 485

With Walter Ewing Crum, *The Conflict of Severus, Patriarch of Antioch, by Athanasius* ("Patrologia orientalis," IV, 569–726) (Paris: Firmin-Didot, 1908)

With Martin Sprengling, *A Descriptive Catalogue of Manuscripts in the Libraries of the University of Chicago* (Chicago: University of Chicago Press, 1912) xi, 128

With Ernest DeWitt Burton, *A Harmony of the Synoptic Gospels for Historical and Critical Study* (New York: Charles Scribner's Sons, 1917) xv, 275

With David Meuli, *Untersuchungen über einige Papyrusfragmente einer griechischen Dichtung* (Zürich, 1920) iii, 42

With Ernest DeWitt Burton, *A Harmony of the Synoptic Gospels in Greek* (Chicago: University of Chicago Press, 1920) xxx, 316

With Shailer Mathews, *The Student's Gospels: A Harmony of the Synoptics, the Gospel of John* (Chicago: University of Chicago Press, 1927) ix, 193 (2d ed. 1934) xiv, 252

With Thomas Wakefield Goodspeed and Charles T. B. Goodspeed, *William Rainey Harper, First President of the University of Chicago* (Chicago: University of Chicago Press, 1928) xi, 241

With Donald W. Riddle and Harold R. Willoughby, *The Rockefeller McCormick New Testament* (Chicago: University of Chicago Press, 1932; 3 vols.) lvi, 124; xiv, 210; xlvi, 370

With J. M. Powis Smith, *The Bible: An American Translation* (Chicago: University of Chicago Press, 1931) xxii, 2038 (Rev. ed. 1935)

With J. M. Powis Smith, *The Short Bible: An American Translation* (Chicago: University of Chicago Press, 1933) x, 545 (Modern Library ed., New York: Random House, 1940)

With Ernest Cadman Colwell, *A Greek Papyrus Reader, with Vocabulary* (Chicago: University of Chicago Press, 1935) ix, 108

With J. M. Powis Smith, *The Complete Bible: An American Translation* (Chicago: University of Chicago Press, 1939) xxvi, 1332

ARTICLES

"A Twelfth-Century Gospels Manuscript," *Biblical World* 10 (1897) 277–80
"The Ayer Papyrus: A Mathematical Fragment" (with plate), *American Journal of Philology* 19 (1898) 25–39
"The Washîm Papyrus of Iliad Theta, 1–68" (with plate), *AJA* 2 (1898) 347–56
"The Newberry Gospels," *AJT* 3 (1899) 116–37
"The Oxford Summer Meeting," *Biblical World* 14 (1899) 446–49
"From Haifa to Nazareth," *Biblical World* 16 (1900) 407–13
"Pappiscus and Philo," *AJT* 4 (1900) 796–802
"A Papyrus Fragment of Iliad E" (with plate), *American Journal of Philology* 21 (1900) 310–14
"The Acts of Paul and Thekla," *Biblical World* 17 (1901) 185–90

"The Book of Thekla," *AJSL* 17 (1901) 65–95
"The City of Herod," *Biblical World* 18 (1901) 88–95
"An Early Christian Letter from Rome," *Biblical World* 18 (1901) 222–24
"An Early Christian Prayer," *Biblical World* 18 (1901) 309–11
"The Textual Value of the Newberry Gospels," *AJT* 5 (1901) 752–55
"From Tiberias to Tabor," *Standard* 49 (1902) 1416–17
"The Haskell Gospels," *JBL* 21 (1902) 100–7
"How Ancient Records Are Dug Out of the Sands of Egypt," *Chicago Tribune* 61, No. 320 (1902) 42
"Karanis Papyri," in *Studies in Classical Philology* (Chicago: University of Chicago Press, 1902) 3, 1–66
"A Martyrological Fragment from Jerusalem," *American Journal of Philology* 23 (1902) 68–74
"Alexandrian Hexameter Fragments," *JHS* 23 (1903) 237–47
"The Ayer Papyrus," *American Mathematical Monthly* 10 (1903) 133–35
"Berlin Papyri 810, 811," in *Aegyptische Urkunden aus den Koeniglichen Museen zu Berlin: Griechische Urkunden* (Berlin: Weidmannsche Buchhandlung, 1903) 125–26
"The Book with Seven Seals," *JBL* 22 (1903) 70–74
"Did Alexandria Influence the Nautical Language of St. Luke?" *Expositor* 8 (1903) 130–41
"Digging Up Ancient Egypt with Prof. Flinders Petrie at Abydus," *Chicago Record-Herald* January 18, 1903, sec. 6, p. 7
"Greek Papyri from the Cairo Museum," *Athenaeum* II, No. 3960 (1903) 387
"A Fourth-Century Deed from Egypt," *Biblia* 15 (1903) 331–37
"The Martyrdom of Cyprian and Justa," *AJSL* 19 (1903) 65–82
"A Medical Papyrus Fragment" (with plate), *American Journal of Philology* 24 (1903) 327–29
"The Oldest Greek Book in the World," *Biblia* 16 (1903) 72–74
"Round about Jerusalem," *Standard* 50 (1903) 1029–30
"The Epistle of Pelagia," *AJSL* 20 (1904) 95–108
"An Ethiopic Manuscript of John's Gospel," *AJSL* 20 (1904) 182–85
"Ethiopic Manuscripts from the Collection of Wilberforce Eames," *AJSL* 20 (1904) 235–44
"Greek Ostraca in America," *American Journal of Philology* 25 (1904) 45–58
"The Madrid Manuscript of Laodiceans," *AJT* 8 (1904) 536–38
"Papyrus Digging with Grenfell and Hunt," *Independent* 57 (1904) 1066–70
"Some Castles in Spain and Other Things: Tangier," *Standard* 51 (1904) 1342–43
"Some Castles in Spain and Other Things: An Old Spanish Capital," *Standard* 51 (1904) 1369
"Some Castles in Spain and Other Things: The Cathedral of Toledo," *Standard* 51 (1904) 1415
"Some Castles in Spain and Other Things: The Escorial," *Standard* 51 (1904) 1543–44
"Some Castles in Spain and Other Things: Granada," *Standard* 52 (1904) 30–31
"Some Castles in Spain and Other Things: The Cathedral of Seville," *Standard* 52 (1904) 135–36
"The Story of Eugenia and Philip," *AJSL* 21 (1904) 37–56
"A Toledo Manuscript of Laodiceans," *JBL* 23 (1904) 76–78
"Ancient Tradition as to the Synoptic Gospels," *Standard* 52 (1905) 1493–94
"A Christian Lamp from Denderah," *Biblical World* 25 (1905) 460–61
"The Dialogue of Timothy and Aquila: Two Unpublished Manuscripts," *JBL* 24 (1905) 58–78
"Fresh Papyri from Oxyrhynchus," *Biblical World* 25 (1905) 228–32
"Greek Documents in the Museum of the New York Historical Society," in *Mélanges Nicole* (Geneva: Imprimerie W. Kündig et Fils, 1905) 177–91
"The Original Conclusion of the Gospel of Mark," *AJT* 9 (1905) 484–90
"How the Russians Celebrate the Epiphany at the Jordon," *Chicago Inter-Ocean* 33, No. 325 (1905) part 6, p. 7
"Bibliography of President Harper's Writings," *Biblical World* 27 (1906) 248–52

"English Beacons of Religion and History: Durham Cathedral—the Shrine of St. Cuthbert,"
        Standard 53 (1906) 983–84
"A Group of Greek Papyrus Texts," *Classical Philology* 1 (1906) 167–75
"The Harvard Gospels," *AJT* 10 (1906) 687–700
"Jesus on the Cross," *Biblical World* 28 (1906) 336–38
"A New Glimpse of Greek Tense-Movements in New Testament Times," *AJT* 10 (1906) 102–3
"An Old Italian Villa: Villa Servelloni," *Standard* 54 (1906) 405–6
"A Part of the Gospel of Matthew from the Beirût Syriac Codex," *JBL* 25 (1906) 58–81
"Tertag and Sarkis: An Armenian Folk-Tale, Translated from the Ethiopic," *American Anti-
        quarian* 28 (1906) 133–40
"Uncle Remus and Hindu Folklore," *Standard* 53 (1906) 1198
"Denison at the University of Chicago," *Denisonian* November 13, 1907, 1, 4–5
"Field Museum Inscriptions," *Classical Philology* 2 (1907) 277–80
"Greek Ostraca in the Haskell Museum," *AJA* 11 (1907) 441–44
"Impressions of Present Day Spain," *Standard* 54 (1907) 1405–6
"Two Supposed Hebraisms in Mark," *Biblical World* 29 (1907) 311–12
"The Detroit Manuscripts of the Septuagint and New Testament," *Biblical World* 31 (1908)
        218–26
"Greek Life from the Papyri," *Outlook* 89 (1908) 566–71
"Karanis Accounts," *Classical Philology* 3 (1908) 428–34
"New Biblical Manuscripts for America," *Independent* 65 (1908) 596–601
"The New Gospel Fragment from Oxyrhynchus," *Biblical World* 31 (1908) 142–46
"A Paris Fragment of Pseudo-Chrysostom," *AJT* 12 (1908) 443–44
"The Syntax of I Cor. 7:18, 27," *AJT* 12 (1908) 249–50
"The Freer Gospels and Shenute of Atripe," *Biblical World* 33 (1909) 201–6
"The Greek Text of Mark 7:11," *ExpTim* 20 (1909) 471–72
"The Nestorian Tablet," *Biblical World* 33 (1909) 279–82
"New Textual Materials from Oxyrhynchus," *Biblical World* 33 (1909) 344–46
"Notes on the Freer Gospels," *AJT* 13 (1909) 597–603
"The Teima Stone," *Biblical World* 33 (1909) 424–25
"The Epistles to the Thessalonians," *Biblical World* 34 (1909) 48–56
"Paul's Voyage to Italy," *Biblical World* 34 (1909) 337–45
"Biblical Texts from the Papyri," *Biblical World* 36 (1910) 67–68
"A Famous Town of Normandy," *Standard* 57 (1910) 1533
"The Freer Manuscripts of Deuteronomy-Joshua," *Biblical World* 36 (1910) 204–9
"The Harrison Papyri," *Classical Philology* 5 (1910) 320–22
"A Lost Manuscript of Justin," *ZNW* 11 (1910) 243–44
"The Old University of Chicago in 1867," *Journal of the Illinois State Historical Society* 3
        (1910) 52–57
"First Clement Called Forth by Hebrews," *JBL* 30 (1911) 157–60
"A Fourth-Century Odyssey," *Classical Journal* 7 (1911) 185–86
"Professor Sanders' Deuteronomy-Joshua," *Biblical World* 37 (1911) 199
"The New Testament of 1611, as a Translation," *Biblical World* 37 (1911) 271–77
"The Making of the New Testament," *Biblical World* 37 (1911) 379–90
"New Testament Manuscripts in America," *Biblical World* 37 (1911) 420–24
"The Toronto Gospels," *AJT* 15 (1911) 268–71
"The Text of the Toronto Gospels," *AJT* 15 (1911) 445–59
"Caspar René Gregory," *Biblical World* 38 (1911) 350–54
"The Vocabulary of Luke and Acts," *JBL* 31 (1912) 92–94
"The Washington Manuscript of the Gospels," *AJT* 17 (1913) 240–49
"The Freer Gospels," *AJT* 17 (1913) 395–411, 599–613; 18 (1914) 131–46, 266–81
"Professor Harnack and the Paris Manuscript of Justin," *AJT* 17 (1913) 411–16

"Appreciation of E. Asada," *University of Chicago Magazine* 7, No. 2 (1914) 21
"A New Testament Anniversary: 1514–1914," *Biblical World* 43 (1914) 164–67
"The Divinity School," *University of Chicago Magazine* 7, No. 5 (1915) 133–41
"Ostraca," in *The International Standard Bible Encyclopaedia* (Chicago: Howard-Severance Co., 1915) 4, 2202–3
"Papyri," in *The International Standard Bible Encyclopaedia* (Chicago: Howard-Severance Co., 1915) 4, 2238–43
"Recent Discoveries in Early Christian Literature," *Biblical World* 46 (1915) 339–48
"Riches and Life," in T. G. Soares (ed.), *University of Chicago Sermons* (Chicago: University of Chicago Press, 1915) 219–30
"The Salutation of Barnabas," *JBL* 34 (1915) 162–65
"The Gospel of John," *Biblical World* 48 (1916) 255–60, 319–25, 382–87; 49 (1917) 57–62, 127–34
"A Letter of Gissing's," *Nation* 103 (1916) 154
"Some Cartoons on the University," *University of Chicago Magazine* 8, No. 4 (1916) 145–50
"The Study of the New Testament" (with Ernest D. Burton), in G. B. Smith (ed.), *A Guide to the Study of the Christian Religion* (Chicago: University of Chicago Press, 1916) 163–238
"The Life of Adventure," *Atlantic Monthly* 120 (1917) 230–35
"A Patristic Parallel to I Corinthians 7:18, 21," *JBL* 36 (1917) 150
"Do One and One Make Two?" *Atlantic Monthly* 122 (1918) 498–502
"The Date of Acts," *Expositor* 17, No. 101 (8th ser., 1919) 387–91
"The House of the Mind," *Atlantic Monthly* 123 (1919) 344–48
"The Original Conclusion of Mark," *Expositor* 18, No. 104 (8th ser., 1919) 155–60
"Sufficient unto the Day," *Expositor* 18, No. 108 (8th ser., 1919) 469–72
"The Week-ender," *Atlantic Monthly* 124 (1919) 204–8; reprinted in B. E. Ward (ed.), *Essays of Our Day* (New York: D. Appleton & Co., 1929) 277–85
"The Origins of Acts," *JBL* 39 (1920) 83–101
Articles in Shailer Mathews and Gerald Birney Smith (eds.), *A Dictionary of Religion and Ethics* (New York: Macmillan, 1921); of the thirty-eight articles contributed, twenty-five were signed: "Barlaam and Joasaph (or Josaphat)"; "Baur, Ferdinand Christian"; "Catacombs"; "Clement of Alexandria"; "Concordance"; "Coptic Church"; "Descent to Hades"; "Didache, The"; "Fathers, Church"; "Glosses"; "Gospels, The"; "Harmony of the Gospels"; "Hasidaeans, Hasidim"; "Hermas, Shepherd of"; "Ignatius"; "Irenaeus"; "Jerome"; "Logia"; "Manuscripts of the Bible"; "Papyrus, Papyri"; "Pastoral Letters"; "Patristics"; "Pseudepigrapha"; "Syrian Church"; "Tertullian"
"Things Seen and Heard," *Atlantic Monthly* 128 (1921) 357–63; reprinted in *Atlantic Classics: Second Series* (Boston: Atlantic Monthly Co., 1928) 122–33
"Chicago, University of," in *The Encyclopaedia Britannica* (12th ed.) (New York: Encyclopaedia Britannica, Inc., 1922) 30, p. 647
"The New Barbarism," *Atlantic Monthly* 130 (1922) 368–72
"The Ghost of King James," *Atlantic Monthly* 133 (1924) 71–76
"The Bible and the Middle-Aged," *Literary Review* 5, No. 27 (1925) 1–2
"Buying Happiness," *Atlantic Monthly* 136 (1925) 343–47; reprinted in W. M. Tanner and D. B. Tanner (eds.), *Modern Familiar Essays* (Boston: Little, Brown & Co., 1927) 242–50, and in A. C. Baugh, P. C. Kitchen and M. W. Black (eds.), *Writing by Types* (New York: D. Appleton-Century Co., 1937) 413–21
"El Placer de Comprar," *Inter-America* 9 (1925) 341–46
"President Burton," *University Record* 11 (1925) 169–73
"William Tyndale and the English New Testament," *Homiletic Review* 90 (1925) 347–51
"The Challenge of New Testament Study," *JR* 6 (1926) 561–69; reprinted in *Divinity Student* 3 (1926) 69–77

"The Manuscripts of the New Testament," "The Language of the Original New Testament," "Papyrus Discoveries" and "Recovery of an Ancient Christian Literature," in *An Outline of Christianity*, Vol. 4: *Christianity and Modern Thought* (New York: Bethlehem Publishers, Inc., 1926) 395–425

"The Magic Carpet," *Knox Alumnus* 11 (1928) 72–78

"The Symbolism of the Joseph Bond Chapel," *Divinity Student* 5 (1928) 13–24

"The Art of Being Outshone," *Atlantic Monthly* 144 (1929) 801–5; reprinted in *Reader's Digest* 18 (1930) 865–67; in B. A. Heydrick (ed.), *Familiar Essays of Today* (New York: Charles Scribner's Sons, 1930) 121–32; in R. W. Pence (ed.), *Essays of Today* (New York: Macmillan, 1935) 216–23; and in F. K. Del Plaine and A. G. Grandy (eds.), *Current Prose for College Students* (New York: Macmillan, 1931) 283–91

"The Chancel Window in the Joseph Bond Chapel," *Divinity Student* 6 (1929) 23–27

"The New Testament," *Chicago Theological Seminary Register* 19, No. 1 (1929) 7–10; reprinted in *Christian Education* 12 (1929) 558–63

"Foreign Lecturers," *Improvement Era* 34, No. 1 (1930) 5–8

"One Year's Progress in New Testament Manuscripts," *University of Chicago Magazine* 22 (1930) 137–42

"The Place of Ephesians in the First Pauline Collection," *ATR* 12 (1930) 189–212

"Keys to Lost Locks," *Improvement Era* 34, No. 10 (1931) 586–87, 623–24

"The Uses of Adversity," *Atlantic Monthly* 148 (1931) 615–20; reprinted in R. W. Pence (ed.), *Readings in Present-Day Writers* (New York: Macmillan, 1933) 399–406

"A Candle for Saint Boniface," *Atlantic Monthly* 149 (1932) 598–601

"Martyrs All!" *Atlantic Monthly* 150 (1932) 495–98

"The Translators to the Reader," *Religion in Life* 1 (1932) 407–18

"The Elizabeth Day McCormick Apocalypse," *JBL* 52 (1933) 81–82

"John Merlin Powis Smith," *AJSL* 49 (1933) 87–96

"A Footnote to Daisy Miller!" *Atlantic Monthly* 153 (1934) 252–53

"The Original Language of the Gospels," *Atlantic Monthly* 154 (1934) 474–78; reprinted in T. S. Kepler (ed.), *Contemporary Thinking about Jesus* (New York: Abingdon-Cokesbury Press, 1944) 58–63

"The Shulammite," *AJSL* 50 (1934) 102–4

"The Marcan Redactor," in L. G. Leary (ed.), *From the Pyramids to Paul: Studies in Honor of George Livingstone Robinson* (New York: Thomas Nelson & Sons, 1935) 57–66

"Miles Coverdale and the English Bible," *Publishers' Weekly* 128 (1935) 805–8

"The Twilight of the Professors," *Atlantic Monthly* 156 (1935) 210–14

"The World's Oldest Bible," *JBL* 54 (1935) 126

"The New Monasticism," *Harper's Monthly Magazine* 173 (1936) 554–56

"A Flier in Fiction," *Improvement Era* 40 (1937) 346–47, 397–99

"The Bible Is News," *Chicago Daily News* December 4, 1940; reprinted in *JBR* 9 (1941) 39

"The Challenge of New Testament Study," *Christian Review* 9, No. 2 (1940); reprinted in *Religious Digest* 11, No. 58 (1940) 7–10

"The Growth of the Bible," *Adult Bible Class Monthly* 33 (1940) 339–46, 375–82, 403–10

"A Complete Bible," *JBR* 9 (1941) 35–38

"How They Came To Translate the New Testament," (with James Moffatt), *International Journal of Religious Education* 17 (1941) 19; reprinted in *Religious Digest* 12 (1941) 5–6

"On Being Dull without a Manuscript," *Atlantic Monthly* 167 (1941) 502–3

"The Possible Aramaic Gospel," *JNES* 1 (1942) 315–40

"The Misprint That Made Good," *Religion in Life* 12 (1943) 205–10

"Paul and Slavery," *JBR* 11 (1943) 169–70

"Greek Idiom in the Gospels," *JBL* 63 (1944) 87–91

"The Didache, Barnabas, and the Doctrina," *ATR* 27 (1945) 228–47

"The Editio Princeps of Paul," *JBL* 64 (1945) 193–204

Articles in Vergilius Ferm (ed.), *An Encyclopedia of Religion* (New York: Philosophical Library, 1945); nineteen articles as follows: "Acts of the Apostles"; "Apologists, Early Christian"; "Canon, Old and New Testament"; "Corinthians, First and Second Letters to the"; "Didache, The"; "Galatians, Letter to the"; "James, Letter of"; "Jude, Letter of"; "Luke, Gospel of"; "Mark, Gospel of"; "Matthew, Gospel of"; "Onesimus"; "Papyrus, Papyri"; "Peter, First and Second Letters of"; "Philemon, Letter to"; "Publication, Early Christian"; "Revelation of John"; "Romans, Letter to the"; "Thessalonians, First and Second Letters to the"

"The Date of Commodian," *Classical Philology* 41 (1946) 46–47

"The Making of the New Testament: Greek and Roman Factors," in *An Introduction to the Revised Standard Version of the New Testament* (New York: International Council of Religious Education, 1946) 31–36

"A Reply," *JBL* 65 (1946) 405–6

"Christmas in Morgan Park Seventy Years Ago," *Chicago Sunday Tribune* 106, No. 51 (1947) part 4, p. 12

"Eight Men and the Bible," *Girls Today* 6, No. 11 (1947) part 5, pp. 4–5; reprinted in *Upward* April 25, 1948, 10–11

"The Marriage at Cana in Galilee," *Int* 1 (1947) 486–89

"Thomas Jefferson and the Bible," *HTR* 40 (1947) 71–76

"In the Beginning," *Religion in Life* 17 (1947–48) 17–22

"New Light on the New Testament," *RevExp* 45 (1948) 155–68

"New Year's Day in Honolulu," *University of Chicago Magazine* 40, No. 2 (1948) 8–9

"The Versions of the New Testament," *Int* 3 (1949) 62–77

"Gaius Titius Justus," *JBL* 69 (1950) 382–83

"The Present State of Bible Translation," *JBR* 18 (1950) 99–100

"Ephesians and the First Edition of Paul," *JBL* 70 (1951) 285–291

"Phoebe's Letter of Introduction," *HTR* 44 (1951) 55–57

"Problems of New Testament Translation," *BT* 3 (1952) 68–71

"The Problem of Hebrews," *JBR* 22 (1954) 122

"Some Greek Notes," *JBL* 73 (1954) 84–92

"Was Theophilus Luke's Publisher?" *JBL* 73 (1954) 84

"Paul," *Look* 20 (December 25, 1956) 26–38 d